Harriet Baskas

111 Places in Seattle That You Must Not Miss

Photographs by Cortney Kelley

emons:

For my brothers, David and Elliot. (Finally, right?)
Harriet Baskas

© Emons Verlag GmbH
All rights reserved
© Photographs by Cortney Kelley, except see p. 238
© Cover icon: shutterstock.com/Anuchart Sungthong
Layout: Eva Kraskes, based on a design
by Lübbeke | Naumann | Thoben
Maps: altancicek.design, www.altancicek.de
Basic cartographical information from Openstreetmap,
© OpenStreetMap-Mitwirkende, OdbL
Editing: Karen E. Seiger
Printing and binding: Grafisches Centrum Cuno, Calbe
Printed in Germany 2023
ISBN 978-3-7408-1992-7
Revised second edition, April 2023

Guidebooks for Locals & Experienced Travelers
Join us in uncovering new places around the world at
www.111places.com

Foreword

Sure, Seattle is known for having lots of rain, more than 800 coffee shops, and, some might say, too many tech workers. But "The Emerald City" is also green year-round. It is the birthplace of innovation and creativity – Jimi Hendrix, grunge music, the cordless phone, not to mention Amazon, Boeing, and Starbucks. You'll find mention of all these stories on these pages, so I won't go on about the creativity and inventiveness inspired by the weather, the caffeine, and proximity to breathtaking nature.

I will take a moment, however, to highlight some of the places I hope this guidebook will entice you to visit or, as it did for me, to revisit with fresh eyes. I knew, for example, that hilly Seattle has hundreds of public stairways, but I didn't know one was haunted, or that beside another is a hidden garden with a fairytale founding story. Over the years, I watched the topiary dinosaurs in Fremont take shape, but I didn't know there were official "dino wranglers." Or that the world headquarters of geocaching was nearby, just past the bronze statue honoring Seattle's favorite clown, J. P. Patches, and his pal, Gertrude.

I'd heard of the Silent Reading Party at the Hotel Sorrento, but I didn't know we could yell and scream all we want while taking a sledgehammer to bottles, TVs, toilets, and more at Rage Industry. I know cooking and dancing classes are popular in Seattle, but not that we could sign up for one-off classes in curling, trapeze art, and forging – even on a date. Or that we could learn fun facts about poop and farts from the Pacific Science Center's *Grossology*-themed bathrooms.

Here you'll find 111 places in Seattle that I don't want you to miss, each with a bonus tip of someplace cool nearby or somehow related. There wasn't room to include every place on my list, but I hope you discover new corners of the city and that you'll share great tips of your own.

111 Places

1___ Acacia Memorial Park
Grand mausoleum with acres of stained glass | 10

2___ Aerocar
This cute car could fly above traffic | 12

3___ Arctic Club Hotel
A Gold Rush club left this gem behind | 14

4___ Art at the Airport
SEA's museum-quality collection | 16

5___ The Arthur Foss
The oldest wooden tugboat was a movie star | 18

6___ Ballard Locks
Engineering marvel, fish ladder, botanical garden | 20

7___ Ballyhoo Curiosity Shop
Head here for taxidermy possum butts | 22

8___ Black Coffee Northwest
Blending with the community over a Melanin Mocha | 24

9___ Boeing Field
Measure the history and wonder of flight | 26

10___ Boeing's First Flight
The B&W Bluebill flew from here in 1916 | 28

11___ Cafe Racer & OBAMA Museum
Live music, a radio station, and really bad art | 30

12___ Capitol Hill Wishing Tree
Leaves of wishes left by passersby | 32

13___ Center for Wooden Boats
Row, row, row a boat or go for a free Sunday sail | 34

14___ Chihuly's Odd Collections
Colorful, curated, and quite kitschy | 36

15___ College Inn Pub
Howard haunts a historic basement pub | 38

16___ Colman Pool
Swim in a saltwater pool with Puget Sound views | 40

17___ Connections Museum
The history of hookups and hang-ups | 42

18___ Dialysis Museum
Chronicling the kidney failure fight | 44

19 — Dino and Dora
Fremont's adorable, adopted, ivy apatosauruses | 46

20 — Dunn Gardens
When the Olmsted Brothers went west | 48

21 — Duwamish Tribal Longhouse
An ancestral site of Seattle's First People | 50

22 — Easy Street Records
Music, meals, cocktails, and more | 52

23 — The Edgewater Hotel
The Beatles slept here, and so can you | 54

24 — Edith Macefield's House
Seattle's famous holdout house | 56

25 — Elliott Bay Marina Dock Six
Free boat ride to a hidden, million-dollar view | 58

26 — Emerald City Trapeze Arts
Fly, get fit, join the circus for a little bit | 60

27 — Exclusion Memorial
First Japanese Americans exiled to camps | 62

28 — Fair Isle Brewing
Coffee shmoffee – drink the beer | 64

29 — Fantagraphics
Visual storytelling at its finest | 66

30 — FareStart Café
Caffeinate for a cause at this nonprofit café | 68

31 — Fast Penny Spirits
A sweet, women-owned bittersweet distillery | 70

32 — Filson Flagship Store
Rugged gear made here, and a meat-vending machine | 72

33 — First Gas Station
Roadside plaque honors a new way to fuel cars | 74

34 — Fishermen's Memorial
Honoring those lost at sea | 76

35 — Former Ford Factory
Model Ts moved along a multi-story assembly line | 78

36 — Geocaching Headquarters
Mecca for modern treasure hunters | 80

37 — Georgetown Steam Plant
Engineering marvel and electrical time machine | 82

38 — Georgetown Trailer Park Mall
A hip place to shop, snack, or get hitched | 84

39____ Gessner Mansion
A gambler's haunted home | 86

40____ Giant Shoes Peep Show
Footwear to fit giants | 88

41____ Grand Illusion
Eclectic films reel out in a quirky space | 90

42____ Granite Curling Club
Not just shuffleboard on ice | 92

43____ Great Wheel
Great spot for a spin or a proposal | 94

44____ Greenest Office Building
Six floors of eco-goodness and sustainability | 96

45____ Green Lake Murder Site
Enjoy your picnic, but remember Sylvia | 98

46____ Greenwood Pencil Box
Supplies for creativity that support good causes | 100

47____ Grossology Bathrooms
Lessons in the loos | 102

48____ Hat 'n' Boots
A supersized howdy for visitors to Oxbow Park | 104

49____ Hot Tub Boats
Rub-a-dub-dub, tour the lake in a tub | 106

50____ Howe Street Stairs
Seattle's longest staircase is quite a workout | 108

51____ International Fountain
Seattle Center's water feature has its own DJ | 110

52____ Ivar's Salmon House
Spot the oosiks | 112

53____ Jimi Hendrix Gravesite
The rock icon's final resting place | 114

54____ J. P. Patches Statue
Celebrating Seattle's favorite clowns | 116

55____ KEXP Gathering Space
Watch radio, drink coffee, see a show, buy records | 118

56____ Kirke Park
Resurrected, but not as planned | 120

57____ Klondike Gold Rush Park
Seattle struck gold with miners heading north | 122

58____ KOBO at Higo
An homage to what came before | 124

59   Kubota Garden
A life, a home, and a garden built and rebuilt | 126

60   Kurt Cobain Benches
Unofficial memorial to grunge music icon | 128

61   Lake View Cemetery
Bruce and Brandon Lee's final resting place | 130

62   Last Resort Fire Department
Where to get fired up in Pioneer Square | 132

63   Lawless Forge
Hammer out a souvenir or a relationship | 134

64   Maury Island UFO Mural
Artwork tells the story of an odd encounter | 136

65   Metsker Maps
Largest retail map shop in the US | 138

66   Murder Mementos
Serial killer souvenirs and bits of bygone clowns | 140

67   NW African American Museum
Celebrating African American culture in the PNW | 142

68   Off the Rez Café
Modern spin on Native American cuisine | 144

69   Oriental Mart
James Beard Award winner with a side of sass | 146

70   Pacific Fishermen Shipyard
Bounty of Ballard's history in salvaged signs | 148

71   Panama Hotel & Tea House
Unclaimed baggage tells a tragic story | 150

72   Paramount Theater Library
Archive of Seattle's entertainment history | 152

73   Patent Tree
Lots of winning ideas | 154

74   Pilling's Pond
Everything at this pond is just ducky | 156

75   The Pinball Museum
Play through the decades | 158

76   Rage Industry
You're encouraged to bust stuff up | 160

77   REI Flagship Store
Prep for adventure and spot a time capsule | 162

78   Retired Air Raid Tower
A Cold War relic in the heart of Phinney Park | 164

79___ Rubber Chicken Museum
All the wacky stuff at Archie McPhee | 166

80___ Scarecrow Video
Be kind and rewind in the 21st century | 168

81___ Schmitz Preserve Park
Old growth in the city | 170

82___ Seattle Asian Art Museum
Heads of divine bodies and a weeping Buddha | 172

83___ Seattle Chocolate Factory
Where tasting chocolate is an experience | 174

84___ Seattle Meowtropolitan
Sip a catpuccino and adopt your new best friend | 176

85___ The Seattle Room
A deep dive into local history | 178

86___ Sicks' Stadium Site
Homebase to local baseball history | 180

87___ Silent Reading Party
Mum's the word at Hotel Sorrento | 182

88___ Sky View Observatory
Locals prefer these sky-high views | 184

89___ Smith Tower
Seattle's first skyscraper | 186

90___ SoDo Track Art
World's longest curated mural corridor | 188

91___ South Willow Street End
Shoreline access for the rest of us | 190

92___ Space Needle Secrets
Fresh views up top, retro souvenirs below | 192

93___ Spice Bridge
Tastes of the world | 194

94___ The State Hotel
Pike Place Market on the walls | 196

95___ Statue of Liberty Plaza
A little Lady Liberty watches over Alki Beach | 198

96___ Streissguth Garden
Lush hillside with a fairytale story | 200

97___ Suzzallo Library
Hogwarts or the University of Washington? | 202

98___ Ted Bundy's Dormitory
A serial killer slept in McMahon Hall | 204

99___ Two Big Blondes
Oldest, largest, plus-size resale store | 206

100___ Unicorn & Narwhal
Colorful and conjoined carnival-themed bars | 208

101___ Volunteer Park Conservatory
Horticultural Heaven | 210

102___ Waterfall Garden Park
Pocket park marks the birthplace of UPS | 212

103___ Wedgwood Rock
Giant geological souvenir and local landmark | 214

104___ West Boston Staircase
19 scary steps | 216

105___ The Wildrose
One of the last lesbian bars | 218

106___ Wing Luke Museum
The Asian Pacific American experience | 220

107___ Wonderful Whirligigs
Artistic energy transforms electric substation | 222

108___ Woodland Park Zoo
Gorillas and why zoos now have natural settings | 224

109___ Woody Guthrie's Legacy
A fascist-killing guitar at MoPOP | 226

110___ World Flight Monument
The first round-the-world flight started here | 228

111___ Ye Olde Curiosity Shop
Century-old shrine to the world's oddest wonders | 230

1 Acacia Memorial Park

Grand mausoleum with acres of stained glass

Acacia Memorial Park, just north of Seattle in Lake Forest Park, was founded in 1926 by the Greater Seattle Masonic Lodge. Freemasons consider the acacia tree to be symbolic of the promise of rebirth and eternity, so it was easy to name the cemetery after the tree. Running the cemetery proved more complicated. So just one year later, the lodge sold the business to the Burnaby family, who kept watch until 1999.

Today, more than 70,000 people are interred in the 63-acre cemetery dotted with sequoias, spruce, century-old redwoods, and enough tree varieties to make the site a field trip destination for college horticultural classes. Feel free to walk the carefully manicured grounds and contemplate the meaning of life and, of course, death. Be on the lookout for gravesites of politicians, sports figures, and other notable people, such as Microsoft cofounder Paul Allen, long-time Washington senator Warren Magnuson, and noted test-pilot Edmund "Eddie" Allen.

Do not leave without venturing inside the 3.5-acre Acacia mausoleum. At the entrance, a glass exhibit case displays a hand-carved replica of the Taj Mahal, the mausoleum Mughal emperor Shah Jahan built for his favorite wife in the mid-1600s. It is there, the staff explains, because many people do not understand the mausoleum concept, and the model creates the "aha" connection.

The Acacia mausoleum is no Taj Mahal, but it is grand and surprising. Down corridors with garden-inspired names such as Lilac, Rose, and Azalea are 7,708 crypts for caskets and 9,500 niches holding decorative urns with cremated remains. Natural light illuminates the entire building through leaded-glass skylights and 29 massive, stained-glass windows decorated with geometric designs, flowers, and religious images. A second, newer mausoleum nearby features a center atrium with a Japanese garden, a waterfall, and reflecting pools.

Address 14951 Bothell Way NE, Seattle, WA 98155, +1 (206) 362-5525, www.acaciafuneralhome.com | Getting there Bus 522, 65 to Bothell Way NE & NE 153rd Street | Hours Daily dawn–dusk, mausoleum 8am–4pm | Tip A few miles northwest, Shoreline Historical Museum digs into the history of the Forest Park neighborhood (18501 Linden Avenue North, www.shorelinehistoricalmuseum.org).

2__Aerocar

This cute car could fly above traffic

The late Moulton (Molt) Taylor, of Longview, Washington was an inventor, tinkerer, engineer, former navy pilot, and world-class dreamer. He had designed some innovative small airplanes, but in the late 1940s he became obsessed with building a car that could fly. Others had tried and failed or written off the idea as science fiction. But Taylor was one who succeeded.

His invention, which he dubbed the Aerocar, was a tiny, two-passenger vehicle that had a small engine, rear propellers, and a set of wings that could be towed behind the car and easily attached to transform the car into a small airplane. The Civil Aeronautics Administration (now the Federal Aviation Administration, or FAA) certified the Aerocar as airworthy. But despite interest from the Ford Motor Company, the Aerocar never went into full production. Still, people did get to see it fly. Taylor made seven prototypes and production models of the Aerocar. In an early newsreel report about the invention, the announcer exclaimed that with the Aerocar drivers would be able to "change a 60-mile-per-hour, traffic-hampered buggy into a high-flyer in the unlimited highways of the sky."

Around 1960, a Portland, Oregon radio station used an Aerocar for eye-catching traffic reporting. And in 1962 actor Bob Cummings flew his own Aerocar in his TV sitcom, *The Bob Cummings Show*, in which he played a photographer and amateur detective with romantic misadventures. In real life, Cummings gave Aerocar rides to his Hollywood dates, among them, it is said, Marilyn Monroe.

Today, the red Aerocar III can be spotted in the Great Gallery at Seattle's Museum of Flight. But you'll have to search for it. The museum's 3-million-cubic-foot, six-story glass and steel main exhibit hall is home to almost 40 full-size historic aircraft. The tiny Aerocar designed for quick getaways is tucked under the wing of one of the larger planes.

Address 9404 E Marginal Way S, Seattle, WA 98108, +1 (206) 764-5700, www.museumofflight.org, info@museumofflight.org | **Getting there** Bus 124 to E Marginal Way S & S 94th Place | **Hours** Daily 10am–5pm | **Tip** From outside the museum you can watch planes land and take off at King County International Airport-Boeing Field next door (7277 Perimeter Road S, www.kingcounty.gov/services/airport.aspx).

3   Arctic Club Hotel
A Gold Rush club left this gem behind

In the early 1900s, some of the lucky prospectors who struck it rich in the Klondike and Alaska gold rushes created an elite Seattle social group known as the Arctic Club. Their first downtown headquarters was in what is now the Morrison Hotel. But in 1916 the club hired architect A. Warren Gould to design something grander where they could socialize, drink, and make deals.

The Beaux-Arts style Arctic Club building Gould created was arctic-inspired and rich in amenities. Its main corridors were clad in fine Alaskan marble. Twenty-seven tusked, terracotta walrus heads dotted the third-floor exterior. And the terracotta panels covering the building's steel-reinforced concrete frame weren't just off-white, they were the first in Seattle to feature colors – teal blue and ochre. Inside, there was a ladies' lounge, billiard and card rooms, a barber shop, a bowling alley, meeting and sleeping rooms, and a rooftop garden.

Several restorations later, the polar bear over the main entrance is long gone, but the walrus heads remain, as do the framed photos of the men who were club members. The wooden lobby bar was stolen, the story goes, in the dead of night from the previous location and nonchalantly reinstalled here overnight. The 3,600-square-foot, formal dining room is still here too. Known today as the Northern Lights Dome Room, it dazzles with a grand chandelier, carved wood support structures, and a circular wood frieze dense with hand-carved fruits and vegetables. Above it all is a stunning, leaded glass dome ceiling lit to evoke the Northern Lights.

The building may also be haunted. In 1936, Congressman Marion Zioncheck jumped to his death from his office on the 5th floor, landing directly in front of the car in which his wife was sitting. "I haven't seen his ghost," says Andy Spaulding, the hotel's former assistant manager, "but he might visit guests staying in what are now rooms 509, 511, or 513."

Address 700 3rd Avenue, Seattle, WA 98104, +1 (206) 340-0340, www.arcticclubhotel.com |
Getting there Bus D, 4, 24 to 3rd Avenue & Cherry Street; Light Rail to Pioneer Square
(1 Line) | Hours Lobby unrestricted, inquire at front desk about Dome Room | Tip Stop
by the nearby Lotte Hotel Seattle to see the ballroom. Located in a former beaux art
church sanctuary, this space has a 63-foot dome, stained glass windows, and a pipe organ
(809 5th Avenue, www.lottehotelseattle.com).

4__Art at the Airport

SEA's museum-quality collection

Airports are the first and last places most people see when visiting a city, and Seattle-Tacoma International Airport (SEA) goes above and beyond to make a good impression.

The city's vibrant music scene is represented with live concerts on multiple stages every day and a Sub Pop Record Shop filled with CDs, vinyl, and merch. Outposts of popular local restaurants and bars abound. And SEA holds a world record for having the longest structure over an active taxiway: a 780-foot-long pedestrian walkway that is 85 feet above the ground.

And then there is the art. In the late 1960s, SEA was the first airport to set aside money from capital improvement projects to buy art by well-known and emerging international and regional artists. "The early acquisitions were quite brilliant," says SEA senior art manager and curator Tommy Gregory. "Today we would not have the ability to collect works like *Night Flight #1* by Louise Nevelson (Conference Center, mezzanine level), *Star Quarters* by Robert Rauschenberg (Concourse C, near higher number gates), and *York Factory A* by Frank Stella (Terminal A, by A 6)." The collection is worth millions, and strolling SEA is like visiting an eclectic museum with artwork not just on the walls, but on the floors, in bathrooms and nursing rooms, on columns and windows, and even embedded in drinking fountains.

Do not miss the art in the baggage claim area, which includes Norman Andersen's *Rainmaker's Baggage*, a kinetic kabob of vintage suitcases at Carousel 8 that surprises passengers by spinning when baggage arrives, and *Eyes on the World* by Richard C. Elliott, near Carousel 15. More than 6 feet high and 20 feet long, Elliott's colorful light installation is made with more than 4,000 industrial grade, acrylic safety reflectors in a pattern inspired by the corn husk baskets made by Plateau Indians along the Columbia River.

Address 17801 International Boulevard, Seattle, WA 98158, +1 (206) 787-5388, www.portseattle.org/sea-tac, SEAcustomercare@portseattle.org | Getting there Light Rail to SeaTac/Airport (1 Line) | Hours Unrestricted | Tip Enjoy a day at 10-acre Angle Lake Park nearby, with swimming beach, spray park, fishing pier, and picnic shelters (19408 International Boulevard, SeaTac, www.seattlesouthside.com/listing/angle-lake-park/1329).

5__ The *Arthur Foss*

The oldest wooden tugboat was a movie star

A fleet of historic vessels owned by the non-profit Northwest Seaport Maritime Heritage Center and moored at Seattle's Lake Union Park offers a deep dive into the maritime heritage of the Northwest Coast and the Puget Sound.

You'll see the 129-foot-long Lightship No. 83, known as *Swiftsure*, which launched in 1904 and served as a floating lighthouse in several ports. In addition to being the oldest lightship in the country, *Swiftsure* is the only one with its original steam engine. The fishing vessel *Tordenskjold* dates to 1911 and was built in Seattle's Ballard neighborhood. Named for Norwegian/Danish naval hero Peter Tordenskjold, this sturdy, 75-foot halibut schooner is made from fir planks and old growth timber. It fished the North Pacific and Bering Sea for 100 years.

To many, the real star here is the 120-foot-long *Arthur Foss*. It is the country's oldest wooden tugboat and the oldest floating vessel in the Pacific Northwest. Built in Portland, OR in 1889, the year Washington became a state, and launched as the *Wallowa*, the sturdy tug's first job was towing sailing ships across the treacherous bar at the mouth of the Columbia River. During the Klondike Gold Rush (see ch. 57), the tug towed ships and barges as far as Nome, Alaska. Purchased by Seattle's Foss Maritime Company and renamed the *Arthur Foss* after the eldest son of company founders Thea and Andrew Foss, the tug was tapped for a starring role as the *Narcissus* in the hit 1933 film *Tugboat Annie*. That film and several others, including one with Ronald Reagan, were based on a series of short stories about a tough-talking female tug skipper inspired by Seattle's waterfront culture and the Foss family saga. Updated with a diesel engine to replace its steam one, the powerful *Arthur Foss* went on to have many more adventures, including military service during World War II, before retiring in 1968.

Address Historic Ships Wharf, Lake Union Park, 860 Terry Avenue N, Seattle, WA 98109, +1 (206) 447-9800, www.nwseaport.org, info@nwseaport.org | **Getting there** Bus C, 40, 64 to Westlake Avenue N & Mercer Street; South Lake Union Streetcar to Lake Union Park | **Hours** Unrestricted, see website for tour schedule | **Tip** The 1909 historic cruising houseboat M/V *Lotus* nearby hosts dockside tours, afternoon tea, and overnight stays (1010 Valley Street, www.mvlotus.org).

6 Ballard Locks

Engineering marvel, fish ladder, botanical garden

Each year, more than 70,000 vessels, from kayaks, commercial fishing boats and yachts to loaded barges with tugboat escorts, pass back and forth through the Hiram M. Chittenden Locks that connect the fresh waters of Lake Washington, Lake Union, and Salmon Bay with the salty waters of Puget Sound. Built by the Army Corps of Engineers and opened in 1917, the two locks and associated facilities include a spillway and gates to help control the different water levels on each side.

The "show" at the Ballard Locks, as this engineering marvel is commonly known, is entertaining and educational. Boats enter the locks, a gate closes behind them, and a mechanism raises or lowers the water – sometimes as much as 26 feet – to match the level on the other side. All the while preventing sea water from Puget Sound from mixing with the fresh water. Then the opposite gate opens, and the boats continue on their way. This process goes on all day.

But there is more to the show. Between June and mid-October, several species of salmon on their journey from the ocean to spawning grounds upriver pass through the area via a fish ladder that includes viewing windows and interpretive exhibits. On sunny days, arrive at midday, when it is often possible to look down into the water and see a large number of fish waiting to enter the ladder.

The hidden treasure at the Ballard Locks is the seven-acre Carl S. English Jr. Botanical Garden, named for the man who spent 40 years transforming the grounds into an English estate garden with more than 500 species and 1,500 varieties of trees and plants, including many rare specimens.

Learn about the history and workings of the locks, the fish ladder, and the garden in the visitor center and museum (both free). Or take a free public tour from March through November. You can go through the locks yourself on an Argosy Cruises boat tour.

Address 3015 NW 54th Street, Seattle, WA 98107, +1 (206) 783-7059,
www.ballardlocks.com | **Getting there** Bus 44 to NW 54th Street & NW 30th Avenue |
Hours Daily 7am–9pm | **Tip** The casual, no-frills Lockspot Café at the Ballard Locks
entrance has been serving fish & chips, fish sandwiches, and steak and seafood staples from
this spot for more than 90 years (3005 NW Locks Place, www.thelockspotcafe.com).

7 Ballyhoo Curiosity Shop

Head here for taxidermy possum butts

Like a lot of kids, Ryan Robbins grew up collecting things. Pez dispensers and Pokémon cards gave way to music CDs, punk rock ephemera, and then odd – and even odder – thrift shop and estate sale items. As he got older, Robbins was also drawn to natural history museums and to trinket shops, such as Seattle's Ye Olde Curiosity Shop, filled with antique and unusual items. In 2015, he found a way to blend those passions and eclectic tastes by opening Ballyhoo Curiosity Shop. "It's my own micro-museum," says Robbins, "But customers can take home some exhibits."

Not all the exhibits though. Robbins' permanent collection includes a fetching, two-headed calf, three full human skeletons, and a tableau of Victorian songbirds against a painted background. "Some of these things, like our Feejee Mermaid, are quintessential sideshow items," says Robbins, with a nod to showman and huckster P. T. Barnum. Other items, like the "Jenny Haniver" – a dried, modified ray or skate like earlier hucksters would pass off as mummified mythological creatures – are here too. "They represent the sort of objects that would have been in every historic oddity shop," he adds.

One of Robbins' favorite spots in the shop is the carefully tended jungle corner, which is home to a menagerie of taxidermy, ranging from a giant moose head and a complete warthog, to opossum and raccoon butts mounted trophy-style. "They may be a bit lowbrow, but taxidermy animal butts are big sellers," says Ryan.

There are more than 10,000 antiques, eccentric items, and gewgaws for perusal in packed aisles that will lead you past pinned butterflies, skulls, jewelry, and fossils, and beneath a chandelier decorated with shrunken heads. Can't decide which treasures to take home? Robbins offers a line of themed mystery boxes, so you can get a running start on your own natural history, rock and mineral, or classic oddities collection.

Address 5445 Ballard Avenue NW, Seattle, WA 98107, +1 (206) 268-0371,
www.ballyhooseattle.com, ballyhooseattle@gmail.com | Getting there Bus 40, 44 to NW
Market Street & Ballard Avenue NW | Hours Daily noon–7pm | Tip In 1906, the city of
Ballard voted to become part of Seattle. The red brick Ballard Centennial Tower at Marvin's
Garden, a tiny wedge-shaped park, contains the bell from Ballard's City Hall, which stood
on the site (5400 Ballard Avenue NW, www.seattle.gov/parks/find/parks/marvins-garden).

8　Black Coffee Northwest

Blending with the community over a Melanin Mocha

Darnesha and Erwin Weary had their first date in a coffee shop more than 20 years ago. Today, they blend a shared love of coffee, their professional experiences, and a commitment to community organizing and community service with their Shoreline coffee shop that doubles as a neighborhood center. "We saw a need for recreation for Black and brown youth and started putting together events," says Darnesha. "And that led us to opening the coffee shop initially because we needed a space to do that work." They also wanted their coffee shop to be a place where people could meet and talk about tough issues and events going on in the city and around the country.

The couple powered through pandemic restrictions, an arson attack a day before the shop's grand opening, and repeated racist vandalism. Nevertheless, they have created a comfortable and culturally inclusive coffeeshop with live edge wood tables, locally made art, and positive messages of social justice. Community-oriented programs include live music, food trucks, after-school homework help, and a Saturday craft marketplace, as well as a free food pantry. They also host an internship program that teaches young people not only marketable barista skills, but also a wide range of financial, business, and other important life and work skills that will be useful throughout their lives.

The drink menu at Black Coffee Northwest is designed to be both entertaining and a community engagement tool. Many of the drinks have alternate names intended to be conversation starters. Here, an Americano coffee is also an Africano; a Cappuccino is also a Blackaccino; and a Chocolate Mocha doubles as a Melanin Mocha. Need a bit less caffeine? Try a Chai Tea Latte by asking for a Supa' Fly Chai. Want something much stronger? Order a doppio espresso by letting the barista know you want to Espress Yo' Self.

Address 16743 Aurora Avenue N, Shoreline, WA 98133, +1 (206) 316-8366, www.blackcoffeenw.com, info@blackcoffeenw.com | **Getting there** Bus E to Aurora Avenue N & N 170th Street | **Hours** Mon–Fri 8am–2pm, Sat 8am–3pm | **Tip** Try a Purple Haze latte at Vietnamese-centered Coffeeholic House. (3700 S Hudson Street or 8585 Greenwood Avenue N, www.timeforcoffeeholic.com).

9 Boeing Field

Measure the history and wonder of flight

In the late 1940s, before Seattle-Tacoma International Airport (SEA) was built, commercial passenger service was handled by King County International Airport (BFI), or Boeing Field.

Named for William E. Boeing, whose company built and tested early aircraft nearby, Boeing Field remains one of the country's busiest general aviation airports, serving cargo flights, private aircraft, and one small commercial carrier, Kenmore Air. Downtown Seattle is just four miles away, so celebrities, dignitaries, and sports teams like to touch down here as well.

The small terminal building, first opened in 1930, has an outdoor viewing area popular with plane spotters, and a grassy area opposite the entrance with several historic plaques. Inside, photo exhibits and a building-wide art collection celebrate the region's ties to aviation history and to the wonder of flight.

Two impressive but easy-to-miss art pieces created for the building's 2003 restoration are right at the front door. The terminal's dark blue terrazzo floor sparkles with stars and other astronomical objects that offer a quick journey from North America to the Moon (at the ticket counter) in Paul Marioni and Ann Troutner's piece, *Our Place in Space*. And be sure to look up. The building's entryway is flanked by Brad Miller's piece, *30,000 Feet*, which uses 30,000 one-foot, metal-edged wooden rulers to represent the common cruising altitude of a commercial flight. Two giant arrows made of rulers point to the ceiling and to a pair of illuminated photographs. One depicts the clouds and sky a commercial flyer might see looking out the window of an airplane flying at 30,000 feet. And, Miller explains, because most flights people take to and from this airport are on small planes, the second photograph is of an evergreen forest as it would look from the window of an aircraft flying at a much lower altitude.

Address 7277 Perimeter Road S, Seattle, WA 98108, +1 (206) 296-7380, www.kingcounty.gov/services/airport.aspx, kciacustsvc@kingcounty.gov | Getting there I-5 S to Albro / Swift Exit 161 | Hours Daily 8am–5pm | Tip The red barn that was the historic birthplace of the Boeing Airplane Company once sat along the Duwamish River, not far from here. The barn is now in the Museum of Flight, across the airfield from the terminal building (9404 E Marginal Way S, www.museumofflight.org).

10 Boeing's First Flight

The B&W Bluebill flew from here in 1916

The Roanoke Street Mini Park is one of almost 150 "street ends" in Seattle that sometimes look like private spaces but are really public rights-of-way that provide access to local shorelines. This tiny, well-tended wedge of a green space is one of the gems. Tucked into a neighborhood of waterfront homes and condos, the mini park has two shaded benches and a pleasing peekaboo view of houseboats, seaplanes, and watercraft on Lake Union.

Easy to miss on the low wall along the park's stone walkway is a bronze plaque noting, "From this site, Boeing launched its first airplane, the B&W, in 1916." The plane was a two-wing floatplane built by William E. Boeing, then a timber executive, avid yachtsman, and budding aviation enthusiast, with his friend and fellow flying fan, U.S. Naval officer Conrad Westervelt. (Thus the "B&W" in the name.) Both men had ridden in Martin seaplanes (Boeing owned one), and together they set out to make an airplane that was better.

Their first plane, the B&W *Bluebill* (Model 1) had a wood skeleton, wire bracing, and a lacquered cloth covering. Parts for the plane were manufactured at Boeing's Red Barn (now a historic aerospace site) and then brought to Lake Union to be assembled in a specially built boathouse.

The B&W *Bluebill* took its first test flight on June 15, 1916 over Lake Union, with Boeing in the pilot's seat. Another test flight took place two weeks later, and a second B&W plane, the *Mallard*, flew from the same spot in November 1916. Boeing tried but failed to sell those first B&W planes and the designs to the US Navy. But he later sold both the *Bluebill* and the *Mallard* to the New Zealand Flying School, which used the planes for training and airmail deliveries. Those two planes are long gone, but a replica of the B&W built in 1966 for the Boeing Company's 50th anniversary can be spotted at Seattle's Museum of Flight.

Address 1 East Roanoke Street, Seattle, WA 98102, +1 (206) 684-4075, www.seattle.gov/ parks//roanoke-street-mini-park | Getting there Bus 70 to Eastlake Avenue E & E Louisa Street | Hours Daily 4am–11:30pm | Tip Kenmore Air offers 20-minute sightseeing seaplane tours over the Seattle metro area from its terminal at the south end of Lake Union (950 Westlake Avenue N, www.kenmoreair.com).

11 Cafe Racer & OBAMA Museum

Live music, a radio station, and really bad art

Before moving to Capitol Hill in 2021, Cafe Racer spent 17 years as a quirky and hip hangout for writers, artists, musicians, and kindred spirits in the University District. Current owners Cindy Anne and Jeff Ramsey are dedicated to maintaining that creative DIY atmosphere. They're current Cafe Racer is larger but equally offbeat in décor and clientele, with live entertainment most nights, karaoke on Mondays, and locally made Pot Pie Factory pot pies on the menu.

A key carry-over from the previous space is the Official Bad Art Museum of Art (OBAMA), owned and curated by Seattle artists Marlow Harris and Jo David. In the earlier Cafe Racer location, there was just an OBAMA room. Now the bad art crawls up the stairs, covers the walls of the mezzanine, and oozes into the bathrooms. "We have some perennial favorites here, such as *Black Velvet Elvis* and *Dogs Playing Poker*. But we also have rarer pieces, such as *Scary Zombie Children* and *Timid Orange Bulldog*," says Harris. Classics, such as *Lobster Lady*(a $5 thrift store find) and *Boob Butt* (a gift from a fan) are back on display, as is *Puppy Slut* and *Jesus of Peeps* (made entirely of, you guessed it, marshmallow Peeps) by artist Janet Galore. One wall features playful, 1960s paint-by-number puppies and kittens. Another is covered in clowns, including "some of the most frightening clown paintings the world has ever seen," says Harris. "We have happy clowns, sad clowns, and one or two Insane Clown Posse wannabes."

Then there are the two bathrooms. Both are open to all. In the pink one with three stalls, "We went totally Hollywood Regency, with gold gilded mirrors, chandeliers, and a dozen old-world paint-by-number pieces," said Harris. In the brown bathroom with urinals, "We went with a darker, gloomier theme, with several brooding portraits and a few fauna horns of conquest, both real and faux." Bad art? You decide.

Address 1510 11th Avenue, Seattle, WA 98122, +1 (206) 905-4383,
www.caferacerseattle.com, hello@caferacerseattle.com | Getting there Bus 11 to
E Pine Street & 12th Avenue | Hours Sun–Thu 6pm–midnight, Fri & Sat 6pm–2am |
Tip Four art installations in the north end of Cal Anderson Park and in the plaza
facing the Capitol Hill Light Rail station make up the AIDS Memorial Pathway
(10th Avenue E and Denny Way, www.theamp.org).

12 Capitol Hill Wishing Tree

Leaves of wishes left by passersby

Wishing trees are a folk tradition in many parts of the world. In some countries, people hammer coins into the bark of living or fallen trees to wish for good health. Elsewhere, people seek good fortune by leaving offerings near the base of trees with spiritual or historic importance.

In the United States, wishing trees often have messages scrawled on bits of paper or on tags hanging like leaves from the branches. Portland, Oregon has several wishing trees. And at Yoko Ono's *Wish Tree for Washington, DC*, in the Hirshhorn Museum's sculpture garden, people may tie on written wishes or lean in and whisper them to the branches.

Here in Seattle, a wishing tree in the leafy Capitol Hill neighborhood grants both shade and, it is believed, wishes. Jane Hamel started this wishing tree in November 2014 when she set out some paper and markers by a great old cedar tree on her property. Seattle's soggy weather ruined the early wishes, but today, thousands of laminated wishes scrawled on small manila tags dangle on colorful ribbons from a framework of wires strung below the tree. A hand-drawn sign on a bench below the tree invites passersby to deposit wishes in the painted coffee can dubbed the "golden jar."

If you have not brought your own pre-written wish, you can choose from a supply of note tags and markers that sit on a table nearby. Fill one out and, *over the next few days your wish will be on the tree*, the sign promises, adding that words of gratitude are welcome, in addition to wishes. The sign ends with the declaration, *Something magical happens when we all wish in one place.*

After you've left your wish, read some of the others there. You'll find wishes for a chance to fall in love, a healthy baby, acceptance, housing for all, more travel, inner peace, world peace, the courage to show up, an end to sickness, and the ability to fly.

Address 1251 21st Avenue E, Seattle, WA 98112 | **Getting there** Bus 12 to 19th Avenue E & E Galer Street | **Hours** Unrestricted | **Tip** Double down on your wishes. There is another, less elaborate Wishing Tree in Dearborn Park in South Seattle (2919 S Brandon Street, www.seattlewishingtree.org).

13 Center for Wooden Boats

Row, row, row a boat or go for a free Sunday sail

It began in the late 1960s, when Dick and Colleen Wagner rented out their growing collection of small, traditional, wooden boats that they kept tied up to their houseboat under the Aurora Bridge on Lake Union. Today, the nonprofit Center for Wooden Boats (CWB) is a hands-on, maritime heritage center with a floating livery of historic boats. You are invited to visit and take a boat out for a spin – for free, in many cases.

On shore, CWB's education center houses a maritime-themed art gallery and a boat shop, where the public can watch historic boats getting restored and new wooden boats being built from historic designs. Boating artifacts are displayed too, including a treasured wherry, a light rowboat made by Seattle's George Yeomans Pocock, the renowned 20th-century racing shell designer and builder.

The real action, though, is on the lake. There is no fee to amble out on the docks to peruse the center's livery. Among the traditional and historic vessels, you will see rowboats, sailboats, canoes, double kayaks, and pedal and paddle boats. Most can be rented for very reasonable fees. If you don't know how to sail, row, or kayak, you can take lessons here.

To encourage everyone to experience the bliss of being on the water, CWB has two bonus programs where the public can use boats for free. You can sign up online for complimentary, one-hour peapod rowboat rentals Wednesdays through Sundays. But those in the know get up early to snag a spot in CWB's Sunday Public Sail, a rain-or-shine tradition for over 25 years, when volunteer skippers give free rides on a changing roster of historic steamboats, schooners, yawls, and yachts from the collection. While touring the lake in style, you'll learn bonus boating history. In September, swing by for the Wooden Boat Festival, when boats arrive from throughout the region and welcome visitors on board.

Address 1010 Valley Street, Seattle, WA 98109, +1 (206) 382-2628, www.cwb.org, info@cwb.org | Getting there Bus C to Fairview Avenue N & Valley Street; South Lake Union Streetcar to Lake Union Park | Hours See website for seasonal hours | Tip Find a spot such as Gas Works Park on the Lake Union shore to watch the Duck Dodge. A tradition since 1974, this wacky, informal sailboat race takes place Tuesday summer evenings and has a weekly theme, like pirates or Mardi Gras.

14__Chihuly's Odd Collections
Colorful, curated, and quite kitschy

Fans of Dale Chihuly's fanciful and colorful glass sculptures will encounter his work in more than 200 museums, hotel lobbies, music halls, and other public spaces, and at Chihuly Garden and Glass, a long-term exhibition at Seattle Center.

While well-known for his glass work, the Seattle-based artist is also an avid collector. He has assembled a vast array of objects, ranging from rare Native American baskets and one of the largest privately held troves of Pendleton blankets, to vintage cameras, toy cars and trucks, cast-iron doorstops, vintage matchbooks, and lots more.

The bulk of Chihuly's collections are stored and displayed in his 25,000-square-foot Boathouse, a private working studio and glassblowing hot shop that's open to the public on rare occasions. Selections from the collection, including a wall of those Pendleton blankets, are displayed at Chihuly Garden and Glass. But a visit to The Bar, the attraction's family-friendly cocktail bar and dining spot, is the tastiest and most delightful way to see an eclectic selection of over 25 of Dale Chihuly's quirky personal collections and more than 36 of his drawings.

Inside the café, accordions are suspended from the ceiling. Hundreds of bottle openers are mounted on the walls in both the men's and women's restrooms and in the hallway in between. There are wall displays ranging from vintage plastic radios and cast-iron dogs to chalkware string dispensers. The best part? Most every table is also a deep shadowbox. And each table contains a different, carefully curated selection from Chihuly's collections of dollhouse furniture, fishing decoys, inkwells, fly fishing reels, Bakelite napkin rings, shaving brushes, and other surprise treasures. When The Bar is not busy, you can wander around and see them all. Or simply take a seat and marvel at the space as you enjoy a cocktail or a meal.

Address 305 Harrison Street, Seattle, WA 98109, +1 (206) 753-4935, www.chihulygardenandglass.com | **Getting there** Seattle Center Monorail to Seattle Center | **Hours** See website for hours | **Tip** Chihuly's *Crystal Cascade* in the lobby of Benaroya Hall, home of the Seattle Symphony, includes two glass chandeliers each weighing three tons (200 University Street, www.seattlesymphony.org/BenaroyaHall).

15 College Inn Pub

Howard haunts a historic basement pub

They never wanted to own a bar. But when Jen Gonyer and her husband, Al Donohue, heard the College Inn Pub was closing forever, they stepped in.

Opened in 1974, the pub fills the basement of an English Tudor revival-style building that was built as a hotel for the 1909 Alaska Yukon Pacific Exposition (Seattle's first World's Fair), which was held on the nearby University of Washington campus. Generations of students, professors, and area residents have fond, sometimes blurry, memories of hanging out in the low-lit, laid-back pub with worn wooden booths, pool tables, dart boards, and a fireplace, Gonyer and Donohue among them. So, rather than let the pub perish, the couple teamed up with their friend Seth Howard, a veteran of Seattle's restaurant and bar industry, to become the bar's new stewards. "The College Inn Pub is very important to the history of Seattle and the University District," says Gonyer, "And, oh yeah, it's also haunted."

The pub's ghost is said to belong to Howard Bok, a sailor or a fisherman, depending on the story, who died many years ago in a room in the hotel above. When the pub opened, Howard's ghost moved down there. "The small room in the back of the pub called the Snug Room is where Howard hangs out," says Gonyer, "Sometimes he plays the piano, moves cue balls, makes noise, or knocks things over." Gonyer has not crossed paths with Bok herself. "Maybe it's because I make sure to talk to him. When I'm at the top of the stairs, I call out, 'It's just me, Howard!' before I come down." But no one is taking chances. Look for an original tabletop on a wall in the back that's been saved for newly minted University of Washington PhDs to carve their names – as has been done for over 40 years.

Note the curtained room opposite the entry landing. "I've been told the light is always left on in that room as a way of honoring the 'working women' who once used the hotel," says Gonyer.

Address 4006 University Way NE, Seattle, WA 98105, +1 (206) 547-0997,
www.thecollegeinnpub.com, howardtheghost@thecollegeinnpub.com | Getting there
Bus 65, 255 to NE Campus Parkway & Brooklyn Avenue NE; Light Rail to U-District
(1 Line) | Hours See website for seasonal hours | Tip Visit the nearby Henry Art
Gallery, the state's first public art museum (15th Avenue NE and NE 41st Street,
www.henryart.org).

16__ Colman Pool

Swim in a saltwater pool with Puget Sound views

Forest trails and a paved beach walkway make West Seattle's 135-acre Lincoln Park on Puget Sound a popular destination year-round. In summer, though, the big draw is Colman Pool, a public, outdoor, saltwater swimming pool.

The pool, on the park's point on the shoreline, has been a favorite recreation spot since 1925, when a natural lagoon was transformed into a dirt-sided pool filled with salt water from the sound at high tide, with the help of a wooden sluice gate. In the early 1940s, it was replaced with an Olympic-sized, concrete-and-tile pool donated to the city by the Colman family in honor of civic leader Laurence Colman.

Dedicated July 4, 1941, with an aquatic party that included diving demonstrations and a canoe ballet, the pool is still filled with Puget Sound saltwater. "Each April, the pool is cleaned and repaired," says Wendy Van De Sompele, the aquatic coordinator. "Then, 500,000 gallons of water are pulled into the pool via three wells on the beach." The water is filtered and then heated and maintained at 84 degrees Fahrenheit by high-efficiency, gas-fired boilers. "Some water evaporates and is replaced, but that's the water that stays all summer," says Van De Sompele, who notes that because saltwater adds some buoyancy, Colman Pool is not certified for setting swimming records. The pool has regularly scheduled lap swims, family swims, and recreational swims, so plan your visits accordingly.

For many visitors, the main attraction is the view. A glass wall separates the pool from the beach. "You can see Vashon and Blake Islands, the Kitsap Peninsula, and, on a clear day, the Olympic Mountains," says Van De Sompele. "A parade of wildlife goes by. Sea lions and orcas are pretty regular, but we also see gray whales and humpbacks." And, she adds, one of the best views of all is from the top of the pool's 50-foot-long corkscrew slide.

Address 8602 Fauntleroy Way SW, Seattle, WA 98136, +1 (206) 684-7494, www.seattle.gov/parks/find/pools/colman-pool | **Getting there** Bus C to Fauntleroy Way SW & SW Rose Street | **Hours** See website | **Tip** The outdoor public Mounger Pool in the Magnolia neighborhood features a corkscrew slide and a toddler pool (2535 32nd Avenue W, www.seattle.gov/parks/find/pools/mounger-pool).

17__Connections Museum

The history of hookups and hang-ups

The 1962 Seattle World's Fair, aka the Century 21 Exposition, introduced technological innovations that were oh-so futuristic at the time. One such first was the cordless phone, created to allow patrons to make "Guess where I am?" calls to friends from tables in the rotating restaurant at the top of the Space Needle. Both inventions are on display at Seattle's Connections Museum in Georgetown, along with hundreds of other artifacts from telecommunications history, dating from the Alexander Graham Bell era to today.

History buffs, telephone nerds, and the communications-curious can wander the collection on their own. But the experience is richer if you say yes to a guided tour through the two-story collection, led by a retired telephone company worker or a tech-savvy volunteer with insider knowledge of the equipment. Visitors can snap selfies beside a giant Trimline phone, stand inside a red telephone box airlifted here from London, or dial (yes, dial) a phone number on an old candlestick telephone and watch the call be routed through the 100-year-old, room-sized, mechanical switching system that was once required to make a telephone call from here to there.

It's impossible to see everything here in one visit, but keep an eye out for the payphone with the clamshell enclosure. It was created for the Tiki-style Polynesia Restaurant built on Pier 51 prior to the 1962 World's Fair.

Look for the telephones from the imaginary "Timbuktu" system, created by former Pacific Northwest Bell employee Ted Hewitt with a switchboard and close to 20 different, still-ringing phones dating back to 1895. According to "Switch Witch" Sarah Autumn, who helps maintain the collection, "It was evidently well known among the installers within PNB that if you removed an older phone from somewhere, you were always supposed to offer it to Hewitt before putting it in the junk pile."

Address 7000 E Marginal Way S, Seattle, WA 98108, +1 (206) 767-3012, www.telcomhistory.org/connections-museum-seattle, info@connectionsmuseum.org | Getting there Bus 60, 124 to E Marginal Way S & Corson Avenue S | Hours Sun 10am–3pm | Tip Tech types may want to visit the nearby Boeing Store stocked with aviation and space-related merchandise and gifts (7742 E Marginal Way S, Building 3-825, www.boeingstore.com).

18 Dialysis Museum
Chronicling the kidney failure fight

The Northwest Kidney Centers' Dialysis Museum tells tales of life-saving medical innovations. Kidneys are the bean-shaped organs below your rib cage that clean your blood, filter out waste, and help balance fluids and minerals in the body. You can live with one working kidney, but if both fail, a kidney transplant or dialysis – regular treatments to filter and purify the blood by machine – are the modern-day options for staying alive.

One of the first practical dialysis machines was the Kolff-Brigham artificial kidney, a rotating drum apparatus created in 1948 by Willem J. Kolff, who became known as the "Father of Artificial Organs." The machine had filters made of sausage casing (cellulose) and, like other machines developed during the 1940s and 1950s, it could only be used to treat patients who had acute kidney failure.

Treating chronic, long-term kidney failure became possible in the early 1960s. That's when the University of Washington's Dr. Belding Scribner thought of using a then new material, Teflon, to make a shunt that could be implanted in a patient's arm and used repeatedly to connect to a dialysis machine without compromising arteries and veins each time.

On display at the Northwest Kidney Centers' SeaTac location are an original Scribner shunt and about two dozen dialysis machines used since the 1940s, including early, refrigerator-sized models and a small "suitcase kidney," like the one Philippine president Ferdinand Marcos is said to have secretly used. The exhibit includes a timeline of dialysis-related advances, stories of notable patients, and a history of the Admissions and Policies Committee of the Seattle Artificial Kidney Center at Swedish Hospital, nicknamed the "God Committee." This panel was charged in the 1960s and early 1970s with deciding which patients would be chosen to receive early, scarce, and costly dialysis treatments.

Address 12901 20th Avenue S, SeaTac, WA 98168, +1 (206) 292-2771, www.nwkidney.org/about-us/dialysis-museum | Getting there By car, take WA-509 to S 128th Street (White Center) and continue to 20th Avenue S | Hours By appointment only | Tip A short drive away, you'll find art by noted Northwestern sculptor Richard Beyer and others is in Dottie Harper Park, named for a local advocate for recreation and art (421 SW 146th Street, Burien, www.burienwa.gov/visitors).

19 Dino and Dora

Fremont's adorable, adopted, ivy apatosauruses

In a neighborhood filled with offbeat public art that includes a giant troll under a bridge, a statue of Lenin, and a 53-foot-tall rocket bearing the neighborhood motto, "*De Libertas Quirkas*" ("Freedom to be Peculiar"), two ivy-covered, prehistoric creatures blend right in. Officially named "Dino" and "Dora," but usually referred to simply as "Mama" and "Baby," the topiary Apatosauruses reside on a private patch of grass on the Burke-Gilman Trail, alongside the Lake Washington Ship Canal.

These dinosaurs are not native to this neighborhood. They were born in the late 1990s as a promotion for an exhibit at the Pacific Science Center, and when they were no longer needed they were adopted – for one dollar – by the quirky folks in Fremont. After mustering flatbed trucks and industrial ingenuity to get the 20-foot-tall, 66-foot-long sculptures across town, it was discovered that the ivy had been merely stuffed into the giant wire frames, rather than grown onto them. The greenery would not last. That is when the Fremont Rotary Club stepped up to plant living ivy in the ground and then carefully weave, drape, and coax the vines to cover the huge structure and form this topiary masterpiece. The gardening project has been in progress for more than 10 years.

Stroll around Dino and Dora today, or follow the kids and walk under them. You will find these two, now lush, topiary dinosaurs ringed by low hedges. If you are lucky, you may come across dino wranglers Randy Cryer and Rudy Pantoja Jr. in action. Tasked with dinosaur grooming, these dedicated Fremont Rotary Club members show up regularly with ladders, hand shears, pruners, rakes, extension shears, and protective gear. "We make a good team. Randy climbs, and I critique so that once he comes down, he does not have to go back up," says Pantoja. "And we make sure the site is kept clean so kids can explore."

Address 433 N 34th Street, Seattle, WA 98103 | Getting there Bus 40 to N 36th Street &
Phinney Avenue N | Hours Unrestricted | Tip Continue along the Burke Gilman Trail to
the tasting room and craft cocktail bar at Fremont Mischief Distillery (132 N Canal Street,
www.fremontmischief.com).

20 Dunn Gardens

When the Olmsted Brothers went west

Seattle's public greenspaces include almost 40 parks and playgrounds designed in the early 20th century by the famed Olmsted Brothers firm. Green Lake and Volunteer Parks are examples of the public spaces the firm created for the city. The team also took private garden commissions from wealthy patrons in the state.

Dunn Gardens is one of those projects, and today it is the state's only Olmsted Brothers estate garden regularly open to the public. Arthur G. Dunn came west from New York in 1899 and made his fortune with Seattle's first fish cannery. He bought land on the edge of the city to build a summer retreat for his family, and in 1915, he hired the Olmsted Brothers to landscape the undeveloped parcel. The firm retained many of the site's natural features, including stands of towering Douglas firs, and added the Great Lawn, walking paths, flowering shrubs, and, at Dunn's request, a variety of deciduous East Coast hardwoods, such as beeches and sugar maples.

While the core of the original design remains, the garden has grown and changed over more than a century. After Dunn's death in 1945, the property was divided among his children. A heather berm replaced roses. Two water features were added. And one of Dunn's sons, Edward Bernard Dunn, a noted gardener in his own right, added a woodland garden.

There are now more than 60 heritage trees on the property. Two to seek out on a self-guided or docent tour are the *Magnolia acuminata*, the largest of its kind in Washington state, and the *Magnolia kobus*, which has spring blooms "that create a 'flower house' that can be enjoyed inside and out," says Carolyn Cox, who is the executive director of the trust that now owns and operates the 7.5-acre Dunn Gardens.

You can visit and stroll through the gardens any time of year and enjoy special events that include concerts, twilight strolls, and lectures.

Address 13533 Northshire Road NW, Seattle, WA 98177, +1 (206) 362-0933, www.dunngardens.org, info@dunngardens.org | **Getting there** Bus 28 to 3rd Avenue NW & NW 137th Street | **Hours** Mon–Sat 9am–4pm | **Tip** Nearby Llandover Woods Greenspace hosts gravel-surfaced trails that dip into a ravine and through a rare patch of urban forest (14499 3rd Avenue NW, www.seattle.gov/parks/find/parks/llandover-woods-greenspace).

21 Duwamish Tribal Longhouse

An ancestral site of Seattle's First People

Attend a cultural event or enter a museum in Seattle, and you may see or hear a version of this statement, "We would like to acknowledge that we are on the traditional land of the first people of Seattle, the Duwamish People past and present and honor with gratitude the land itself and the Duwamish Tribe."

The message may make you curious about the people who lived on and cared for the area's land and waterways before white settlers arrived and took it for their own. While currently not one of Washington's federally recognized tribes, the Duwamish People, the region's only indigenous tribe, are very much still here. And they warmly welcome visitors at a cultural center and longhouse across the street from park land on the Duwamish River shoreline that was the site of one of the tribe's largest villages before it was burned down by settlers in 1895.

In addition to a Native art gallery and gift shop, the center displays Edward Curtis prints of early tribal members and archeological objects from the seven-acre *həʔapus* ["ha-ah-poos"] Village Park (formerly the Port of Seattle's Terminal 107 Park), across the street. Some sacred tribal artifacts are displayed here too, including the bark hat that once belonged to Si'ahl (Anglicized to "Seattle"), the Duwamish and Suquamish chief who welcomed and helped the earliest white settlers and for whom the city was named.

Leave time to hike the wooded paths on the hillside behind the center and cross the street to explore the cultural installations on the park site and the viewing spots on the Duwamish River shoreline. You can gain far deeper knowledge of and appreciation for this National Register of Historic Places site by joining one of the center's free walking tours that cover the area's geology, archeology, anthropology, and the history of the Duwamish people.

Address 4705 W Marginal Way SW, Seattle, WA 98106, +1 (206) 431-1582, www.duwamishtribe.org, info@duwamishtribe.org | Getting there By car, take Highway 99 S/WA-509 S to WA-99 S, exit at W Marginal Way/South Park | Hours Tue–Sat 10am–5pm | Tip The Duwamish Trail runs north and south along the industrial Duwamish Waterway, past *həʔapus* Village Park and, to the north, Herring's House Park with views of the river and interpretive signs (4570 West Marginal Way SW, www.seattle.gov/parks/find/parks/herrings-house-park).

22__Easy Street Records
Music, meals, cocktails, and more

"Don't be alarmed if you see a well-known DJ spinning records in the loft," says Matt Vaughn, owner of Easy Street Records, or if you spot a familiar musician thumbing through the vinyl bins. "There are a lot of touring acts that come through town. And, like us, they're all music fans. So, you might look up, and there's Cheap Trick shopping, Isaac Brock from Modest Mouse, Brandi Carlile, or a guy from Pearl Jam. That sort of thing happens regularly."

Easy Street Records is just that cool. The independent record store has been in the same spot at The Junction in West Seattle since 1989 and "is not a spot that just carries new releases and up and coming, trend-setting records," says Vaughn. "We're also purveyors of the Northwest music scene and the history it represents. So, the shop often hosts record release events and listening parties for local bands."

Vinyl fans should make a beeline to the back corner of the upstairs mezzanine and the bin labeled "Today's Treasures." Vaughn calls it "the bird feeder of the store" and says that's where they put the fresh used vinyl arrivals. "It changes every day and is where the rare, collectible, and first pressing will go. So, for the avid vinyl collector or those looking for some deals, I'd say that's the first place to go."

The in-store stage has hosted live performances by everyone from Macklemore, Pearl Jam, and Band of Horses, to Patti Smith, Lou Reed, and Elvis Costello. "We don't book way ahead," says Vaughn, "So check Instagram or our marquee, or ask what's happening when you're in the store."

Grab breakfast or lunch in the Easy Street Café, with its music-themed menu. Try the omelets named for Woody Guthrie, Hank Williams, and Beck; James Browns (hash browns); the Dolly Parton Stack (pancakes); or the easy to carry Born to Run breakfast sandwich. Round out the meal with a cocktail from the upstairs bar.

Address 4559 California Avenue SW, Seattle, WA 98116, +1 (206) 938-3279, www.easystreetonline.com, info@easystreetonline.com | Getting there Bus C, 55 to SW Alaska Street & California Avenue SW | Hours Shop Mon–Sat 9am–9pm, Sun 9am–7pm; café: daily 7am–3pm | Tip Matt Vaughn recommends the cocktail bar inside Maharaja Cuisine of India across the street (4542 California Avenue SW, www.maharajawestseattle.com). "It feels like a speakeasy – it has stiff drinks and a bartender who has been there for 30 years."

23 The Edgewater Hotel

The Beatles slept here, and so can you

Plenty of hotels in Seattle offer water views. But The Edgewater Hotel on Seattle's downtown waterfront is the only one that can boast rooms with over-the-water views of Elliott Bay, thanks to its perch on Pier 67. Built in 1962 for the Seattle World's Fair, the hotel, unfortunately, did not open its doors to paying guests until the fair ended. When it did, it was advertised as the only hotel where you could fish out of your window. To prove the point, bait and tackle were sold in the lobby.

But the Edgewater's real claim to fame is the long list of legendary bands and artists who have stayed here – and the raucous and raunchy stories (many true, some apocryphal) associated with their stays. The most famous guests were The Beatles. The Fab Four stopped in Seattle in August 1964 during their first U.S. tour, when Beatlemania was in full swing. You may have seen the iconic photo of them fishing from their hotel suite window. Led Zeppelin was notoriously banned from the hotel for bad behavior that included chucking TVs and furniture out their hotel room windows. And Frank Zappa namechecked the hotel in recorded songs and live performances, relating tales involving mud sharks and other sea creatures reeled in – also through the windows.

Today's guests can opt to sleep in the same suite The Beatles stayed in or book a night in the Pearl Jam suite, which sports a grunge-inspired design, a Fender guitar and amplifier, a record player, and a selection of vinyl records. Not checking in? The hotel's lodge-like lobby has comfy sofas, two-story windows overlooking the water, and a Hall of Fame corner featuring photos of some of the famous guests who have visited over the years. That list includes everyone from President Bill Clinton and Anthony Bourdain to The Rolling Stones, Elvis Presley, Stevie Wonder, The Monkees, Blondie, Roy Orbison, and Willie Nelson.

Address 2411 Alaskan Way, Seattle, WA 98121, +1 (206) 792-5959, www.edgewaterhotel.com, guestservices@edgewaterhotel.com | Getting there Bus 29 to 1st Avenue & Wall Street | Hours Unrestricted | Tip Learn about mud sharks and other creatures that live in Elliott Bay at the Seattle Aquarium on Pier 59 (1483 Alaskan Way, www.seattleaquarium.org).

24 Edith Macefield's House

Seattle's famous holdout house

Commercial development in her Ballard neighborhood did not impress Edith Macefield. The feisty senior citizen was determined to continue living in her small, two-bedroom home with the white picket fence, even as a hulking, multi-story, concrete shopping center and parking structure was being constructed around her.

Developers offered Macefield $750,000 to move out of the 1,050-square-foot house. She said no. They increased the offer. In 2006, she gained worldwide fame – and loads of fans – when she also turned down $1 million, a new home, and healthcare. She liked this house, which had been built in 1900 and then moved to this spot, she said. She had cared for her dying mother in that home. And she was not interested in moving. "I don't need the money. Money doesn't mean anything," she told the *Seattle Post-Intelligencer*. Instead, Macefield stayed put, construction continued, and the little house was added to the list of famous holdout properties known as 'nail houses' that end up standing alone amid larger real estate projects.

Macefield died in her home on June 1, 2008 at age 86. Before her death, Macefield had actually become friends with the senior superintendent of the Ballard Blocks commercial development that now surrounds the house. And in a storybook twist, she left him the house. Over the years, plans have been floated to move the house or turn it into a coffee shop. Today, the Edith Macefield House stands empty and boarded up. In another odd twist, it's now owned by the real estate company that owns the Ballard Blocks.

While Disney/Pixar's movie *Up* was not based on Edith Macefield's defiant story, the house was used to promote the film, which centers around a man who refuses to sell his home as construction encroaches. He flies the house away with the help of helium balloons. So feel free to leave a balloon tied to the fence.

Address 1438 NW 46th Street, Seattle, WA 98107 | Getting there Bus D, 40 to 15th Avenue NW & NW Leary Way | Hours Unrestricted | Tip Hungry fans of holdouts will enjoy Mike's Chili Parlor around the corner. The dive bar has been serving its meaty signature chili since 1939 (1447 NW Ballard Way, www.facebook.com/MikesChiliParlor).

25 __ Elliott Bay Marina Dock Six

Free boat ride to a hidden, million-dollar view

Elliott Bay Marina, below the Magnolia neighborhood bluffs, boasts of being the largest private marina on the West Coast, with more than 1,200 in water slips, 10 miles of dock, "and a country club environment with panoramic views of the Seattle skyline." True all around. From the path on the marina shore, you can see yachts galore, of course, but also the Space Needle and downtown Seattle, the Olympic Mountains, cruise ships in port, and marine activity on the bay.

The marina opened in 1991 after a protracted planning and permitting process that included negotiations with the Muckleshoot and Suquamish Native American tribes, who argued that the proposed site was in their accustomed, treaty-protected fishing grounds. An accord was reached that requires the marina to give 6% of annual gross revenues to the tribes.

By agreement with the city, the marina also provides a public observation deck out on the breakwater that is a true hidden treasure. Its elevated spot over the water offers unobstructed views of everything you can glimpse from land, and there is rarely anyone else out there. Accessing the deck is an adventure on its own. All marina docks are gated and locked, except for Dock 6, which is open when the fueling station and convenience store is open. Walk down the dock, pop into the shop, and ask for your free ride to the breakwater. It takes just three minutes to board the pontoon boat, motor over, and disembark. The pontoon skipper (aka, the store clerk) will come get you when you are ready to come back.

Access is year-round. "I wouldn't recommend going out there when the wind is blowing 50 miles per hour from the south," says Harbormaster Jordan Glidden. "But in the summer, if you're planning to go out there with a group of friends, feel free to call ahead."

Address 2601 West Marina Place, Seattle, WA 98199, +1 (206) 285-4817, www.elliottbaymarina.co, info@elliottbaymarina.net | Getting there By car, take 15th Avenue W to W Garfield Street/Magnolia Bridge, exit at Elliott Bay Marina/Cruise Terminal | Hours Platform daily 9am–dusk | Tip On the shore, check out Palisade Restaurant's swanky décor and indoor pond. Maggie Bluffs, below, is more relaxed and less spendy with the same views plus a dog-friendly patio (2601 West Marina Place, www.maggiebluffs.com).

26 Emerald City Trapeze Arts

Fly, get fit, join the circus for a little bit

If you're wondering what it would be like to fly through the air with the greatest of ease, as the song goes, or to perform acrobatics with aerial silks, hoops, or ropes, Emerald City Trapeze Arts is a fun, safe place to try it all out. The circus school fills a 20,000-square-foot, timber-frame building in SoDo that once housed a boiler works factory. Today, the space features a full-sized, indoor, flying trapeze rig in one giant hall and a professional grade aerial studio in the other.

Two-hour introductory classes include flying trapeze and aerial skills, as well as acrobatics and circus-style fitness, all taught by world-class instructors and professional circus performers. Participants of all fitness levels (and at least 12 years old) are welcome. What should you wear? Comfortable form-fitting athletic clothes are good. But to encourage the joyousness that exudes from both instructors and students, the students show up in everything from stripes, knee-high socks, and polka-dots, to bow-ties, multicolored tights, and any other circus wear.

That goes for the popular Friday night date classes too, which begin with acrobatic partner yoga. "Don't be surprised when you end up in a compromising position," the write-up all but promises. The action then moves up 30 feet to the flying trapeze platform, where students might be swinging on a bar and hanging by their knees within 20 minutes (with a safety harness, of course). "We get a lot of couples on first dates," says trapeze instructor Samantha Buckmeier, "But also couples celebrating milestone anniversaries."

On many holidays and other times of the year, Emerald City Trapeze also hosts spectacular performances featuring resident and visiting performers and their daring trapeze, aerial, and circus acts. Try to book your ticket for the viewing balcony to get a rare 'fly height' view of the action.

Address 2702 6th Avenue S, Seattle, WA 98134, +1 (206) 906-9442, www.emeraldcitytrapeze.com, info@emeraldcitytrapeze.com | Getting there Light Rail to SoDo (1 Line) | Hours See website for class schedule | Tip Emerald City Trapeze instructors are fans of Derby, a SoDo restaurant and bar located inside The Shop, a private club for car and motorcycle enthusiasts that offers Saturday tours (2233 6th Avenue S, www.derbyrestaurants.com/seattle).

27 __ Exclusion Memorial
First Japanese Americans exiled to camps

The U.S. declared war on Japan the day after Japanese forces attacked Pearl Harbor on December 7, 1941. Two months later, on February 19, 1942, President Franklin D. Roosevelt bowed to prejudice and wartime hysteria when he signed Executive Order 9066, giving the War Department the authority to create zones from which "any or all persons may be excluded." The order did not name specific locations or people, but it was clear that Japanese Americans on the West Coast were intended, regardless of whether they were US citizens.

Some families moved out of the army's prohibited zones. But on March 18, 1942, the government created the War Relocation Authority. Within a week, the first wave of what would be more than 120,0000 Japanese Americans were forced to leave their homes and move to concentration camps (officially "Relocation Centers") in California, Idaho, and other states for the duration of World War II.

Bainbridge Island was the first exclusion zone. On March 30, 1942, 227 Japanese Americans from the island (most of them U.S. citizens) were gathered at Eagledale Ferry dock by armed U.S. soldiers and sent first to a concentration camp in Manzanar, CA and then to Idaho's Minidoka Center. They were given just six days' notice and the proviso that they could bring only what they could carry or wear. They were not told where they were going.

Guided by the mission of *Nidoto Nai Yoni*, or "Let It Not Happen Again," the community built the moving Bainbridge Island Japanese American Exclusion Memorial in a wooded garden area near the historic ferry dock. Onsite is a 276-foot-long, curving wall of old-growth cedar, granite, and basalt bearing the names of those first 227 exiled Japanese Americans, along with five large terracotta murals illustrating personal stories and the community's support. By the dock, a 100-year-old Western Red Cedar is a living 'witness tree' to the evacuation.

Address Pritchard Park, 4192 Eagle Harbor Drive, Bainbridge Island, WA 98110, +1 (206) 660-6350, www.bijaema.org, info@bijaema.org | Getting there Ferry to Bainbridge Island, then take Kitsap Transit bus 99 from ferry dock | Hours Daily dawn–dusk | Tip Learn more about the local Japanese American community at the Bainbridge Island Historical Museum in downtown Winslow (215 Eriksen Avenue NE, www.bainbridgehistory.org).

28__Fair Isle Brewing

Coffee shmoffee – drink the beer

Beyond coffee, Seattle is now well known nationally as a haven for beer enthusiasts. There are around 70 craft breweries throughout the city, each with its own character and unique approach to making and presenting beer.

One square mile in Ballard's light industrial area is home to a cluster of more than a dozen of those breweries. And while their proximity is, of course, convenient for drinkers, it also fuels camaraderie and creativity amongst the brewers themselves, who offer up an ever-changing roster of beers ranging from the traditional to the exotic, with plenty of personal twists mixed in.

At Fair Isle Brewing, they skip the IPAs and focus strictly on farmhouse ales and mixed culture saisons fermented with a special house culture of wild yeast and bacteria, with a rotating selection of flowers, plants, berries, spices, and other ingredients sourced and foraged in Washington and throughout the Pacific Northwest. "We want to create beer that represents where we are in the world and the time," says Fair Isle Brewing Co-Founder Andrew Pogue. "And the cool thing about being in Washington is that we have a vast variety of local producers to work with."

Many states don't have one local maltster, says Pogue, but in Washington, there are many craft maltsters to choose from. "We are not local for the sake of being local, but for the quality around us. It's the same with fruit and berries. The beauty of being in Washington is that you can do this really well, drawing on suppliers from Idaho, Oregon, and British Columbia as well."

In Fair Isle's taproom, you can get a glimpse of the brewery process and see some of the wine barrels and casks used to mature the beer. "Feel free to ask the bartenders to explain the process and make some tasting recommendations," says Pogue. And check the schedule for pop-ups hosted by local chefs testing out new concepts.

Address 936 NW 49th Street, Seattle, WA 98107, +1 (206) 428-3434, www.fairislebrewing.com | **Getting there** Bus 40 to NW Leary Way & 11th Avenue NW | **Hours** Tue–Thu 3–9pm, Fri 3–10pm, Sat noon–10pm, Sun noon–8pm | **Tip** Many breweries are dog-friendly, but Ballard's Dog Yard Bar has an indoor/outdoor, off leash play park for your best friend (1546 NW Leary Way, www.dogyardbar.com).

29 Fantagraphics
Visual storytelling at its finest

If you're a fan of modern comics and graphic novels, you may already be familiar with Fantagraphics. Founded on the East Coast in the mid-1970s and now based in Seattle, the scrappy, independent press is well-known for printing the work of both emerging and recognized cartoonists as part of its mission, "To celebrate great cartooning in all of its incarnations, from the form's early luminaries to contemporary artists currently forging the future of visual storytelling."

The company's eclectic offerings include everything from anthologies of *Peanuts*, Disney, *Pogo*, and other comic classics, to critically acclaimed art comics and graphic novels, such as *Love and Rockets* by Gilbert, Jaime, and Mario Hernandez; *Ghost World* by Daniel Clowes; and Simon Hanselmann's *Megahex*.

In 2006, Fantagraphics opened the doors to a unique bookstore/gallery/performance space in Seattle's Georgetown neighborhood. Fantagraphics' full in-print line is here, along with merchandise, rare and out-of-print titles, and offerings from like-minded publishers, as well as hats, t-shirts, and calendars.

"We take a broad view of publication," says Larry Reid, Fantagraphics store manager and gallery curator, "Part of our mission is to support new and unpublished artists. And one way we do that is to feature their work in our store. So, you will find that many of the books we have here are handcrafted, artist-made editions that may be published only in very short runs."

In addition to book signings, artist talks, workshops, concerts, and other events, the Fantagraphics storefront also serves as a gallery space. Exhibitions change monthly and feature work that is topical, political, and often drawn from newly published titles. "The exhibition space gives people interested in contemporary culture the opportunity to discover new talent and to see original artwork by some great masters of the medium," says Reid.

Address 1201 S Vale Street, Seattle, WA 98108, +1 (206) 557-4910, www.fantagraphics.com | Getting there Bus 124 to Airport Way S & S Vale Street | Hours Mon–Sat 11:30am–8pm, Sun 11:30am–5pm | Tip Fantagraphics shares space with Georgetown Records, a great spot for used vinyl, CDs by local bands, and live music (www.georgetownrecords.net).

30 FareStart Café

Caffeinate for a cause at this nonprofit café

There are plenty of hip coffee shops in the South Lake Union neighborhood, where tech giant Amazon has a multi-building campus. But the FareStart Café, a lobby-level spot open to the public in one of Amazon's office buildings, is the rare bistro where your sit-down or takeaway order does more than give you a buzz and fill your stomach. This is a coffee shop with a mission. It is part of FareStart's goal to transform lives, disrupt poverty, and nourish communities through food, life skills, and job training. The nonprofit, James Beard Award-winning organization provides restaurant industry job training, along with a wide range of practical skills, to adults and young people who have experienced homelessness, poverty, incarceration, and other challenges that can get in the way of getting and often keeping a job. Participants are set up for success with free skills training and additional resources that can include everything from paychecks, housing assistance, and clothing to counseling services and transit passes. 97 percent of FareStart's adult graduates have jobs within 90 days of finishing the program. This full-embrace approach works.

The FareStart Café in South Lake Union is the public-facing social enterprise piece of FareStart's Barista & Customer Service Program for young people experiencing poverty or homelessness, or facing barriers to high school graduation. Beyond real-world job experience and wages, students can earn high school credits, access FareStart's wraparound social service offerings, and acquire skills that will be useful in the workforce and, more importantly, in life.

FareStart Café's locally sourced, market-priced menu includes Starbucks coffee, Gourmondo salads and sandwiches, and pastries from Macrina Bakery. Whipped cream 'pup cups' for your furry friends are not posted on the menu, but they're complimentary if you know to ask.

Address 399 Fairview Avenue N, Seattle, WA 98109 (in Amazon's Houdini North Building), www.farestart.org/farestart-cafe | **Getting there** Bus 70 to Fairview Avenue N & Harrison Street; South Lake Union Streetcar to Terry Avenue | **Hours** Mon–Fri 7am–3pm | **Tip** Get exposed to global health innovations with interactive exhibits at the Bill & Melinda Gates Foundation Discovery Center (440 5th Avenue N, www.discovergates.org).

31 Fast Penny Spirits

A sweet, women-owned bittersweet distillery

During the first year of the pandemic, Jamie Hunt and Holly Robinson, co-founders of Fast Penny Spirits, opened their *amaro* distillery. The duo also debuted a destination tasting deck in a boatyard and collected awards for their Italian-style Amaricano and Amaricano Bianca amari. "Hurray for them," you may be thinking. "But what is *amaro*?"

It is an Italian herbal, bittersweet liqueur traditionally served neat or over ice to treat ailments or, before or after a meal, to aid digestion. It is also a core ingredient in many classic and modern-day craft cocktails, such as the Aperol spritz. But, as Fast Penny describes it, "Amaro has always been a mystical mystery in the spirits world, surrounded by secrecy with few rules."

Fast Penny's rules for making *amaro* include finding that pleasingly sweet and bitter spot between tradition and modernity, plus a commitment to sustainability. They use organic, foraged, and regional ingredients, and they give back at least 3% of their bottle sales to help women in business and other community efforts.

Their amari are made with upcycled grape spirits and reclaimed corks, fair-trade organic sugar, and a secret blend of over 45 botanicals that can be spotted in the carefully labeled glass jars and bottles in the lab at the back of the distillery during tours. The tasty menu of Northwest-sourced ingredients they add to the amari includes everything from black truffle, saffron, Rainier cherries, and hops, to cocoa nibs, hazelnuts, rosebuds, and cascara, which is made from the dried skins of the coffee fruit.

Fast Penny's tasting deck has barrel tables, a roll-up door, a walk-up bar, and a sophisticated, in-the-know vibe due to its location inside a working shipyard on the Queen Anne side of the Ballard Bridge. Be sure to check their social media feeds for curated, pop-up events championing like-minded emerging businesses.

Address 1138 W Ewing Street, Suite B, Seattle, WA 98119, +1 (206) 627-0272, www.fastpennyspirits.com, hello@fastpennyspirits.com | Getting there Bus 29, 31, 32 to W Nickerson Street & 12th Avenue W | Hours See website for seasonal hours | Tip Craft beers and Lake Washington Ship Canal views are all yours nearby at the Rooftop Brewing Company (1220 W Nickerson Street, www.rooftopbrew.co).

32 Filson Flagship Store

Rugged gear made here, and a meat-vending machine

Prospectors rushing north to Alaska and Canada's Yukon territory after 1896 with dreams of striking it rich in the Klondike Gold Rush needed good fortune – and very reliable gear. Luck they had to find on their own. But for the necessary rugged clothing, boots, sleeping bags, and other accessories, one of the outfitters they could turn to in the jumping-off city of Seattle was C. C. Filson's Pioneer Alaska Clothing and Blanket Manufacturers, established in 1897.

After the Gold Rush, the company continued equipping hunters, loggers, cowboys, fishers, and others who spend serious time working and playing outside. The Filson brand remains synonymous with top-quality, durable gear. The company has operated out of several Seattle locations, but its 6,500-square-foot flagship store, which opened in 2013, is an impressive mix of retail store, factory, craft museum, and funhouse for fans of the brand and the outdoors.

Notice the forged wolf-head handles by Darryl Nelson on the front doors. Just inside, large windows offer views of workers stitching Filson products. Along the stairway to the main floor is a 17-foot-tall contemporary totem pole by Aleph Geddis, a giant likeness of Smokey Bear by chainsaw artist Bob King, and a vending machine filled with smoked and cured meat treats from Cle Elum-based Owen's Meats ("The Candy Store for the Carnivore"), which traces its roots back to 1887.

In addition to a large, wood-burning fireplace, copious taxidermy, salvaged tools, and a huge trellis made of lumber from the original Boeing factory, the main retail floor is home to the Filson Restoration Department. This unique workshop is staffed by craftsmen who are happy to chat with you about how they spend their days transforming Filson bags that have been decommissioned or deemed unrepairable into highly sought-after, one-of-a-kind duffle bags, pouches, and other accessories.

Address 1741 1st Avenue S, Seattle, WA 98134, +1 (206) 622-3147, www.filson.com |
Getting there Bus 21 to 1st Avenue S & S Holgate Street | Hours Mon–Sat 10am–6pm,
Sun 11am–5pm | Tip From Filson, head south to Westland Distillery, a well-known
producer of American single malt whiskey, for tastings, tours, and snacks (2931 1st Avenue S,
www.westlanddistillery.com).

33 __First Gas Station

Roadside plaque honors a new way to fuel cars

Early automobile owners could not just pull into a service station and ask an attendant to fill up the tank, wash the windshield, and check the oil. Nor could they slide a credit card into a machine, grab a nozzle, and pump their own gas.

Instead, they hauled fuel home from the general store in 5-gallon cans and filled their gas tanks themselves, most likely with funnels. That dangerous routine changed around 1905, when inventor Sylvanus Freelove Bowser turned his patented kerosene pump into the "Self-Measuring Gasoline Storage Pump." A hose attachment for filling fuel tanks paved the way for another invention: drive-up filling stations. And according to a plaque set on a low concrete pedestal near a Port of Seattle shipping yard, Seattle was the home of the world's first service station. Dated 1947, this plaque reads:

Here in the spring of 1907 an odd but ingenious contraption was erected by the late John McLean of Standard Old Company of California for the unprecedented function of dispensing gasoline and oil directly to a motorist. From this significant pioneer effort came one of the greatest conveniences to the public – the service station.

Several other cities around the country, including Detroit, Los Angeles, Pittsburgh, and St. Louis, also lay claim to being the site of the first gas station. Debate seems to center on whether a 'station' was a single fuel pump or a purpose-built fueling center offering motorists services such as air for their tires in addition to a fill up. So maybe it's a claim that requires further investigation.

For now, Seattle is confident enough about its place in gasoline history to leave the monument where it is. You'll find it in an easy-to-miss spot along a busy road in an industrial part of town with, ironically, few places to park a car. A protected bike lane goes by the site, so consider visiting the plaque honoring the first gas station on two wheels instead of four.

Address 2225 E Marginal Way S, Seattle, WA 98134 | Getting there By car, take Alaskan Way S to Marginal Way S | Hours Unrestricted | Tip Auto enthusiasts might enjoy a short road trip to LeMay – America's Car Museum (2702 East D Street, Tacoma, www.americascarmuseum.org).

34 _Fishermen's Memorial

Honoring those lost at sea

Today, Seattle is well known for its technology industry. But the maritime industry's role in the area's history and economy reaches back more than 100 years, with Fishermen's Terminal serving as homeport for the North Pacific Fishing Fleet. Opened January 10, 1914 as "Fishermen's Headquarters," the terminal remains a place for the commercial fishermen who pursue salmon, halibut, Alaskan king crab, and other seafood in Northwest and Alaskan waters to moor, repair, and provision their boats in the offseason.

Then and now, commercial fishing is an extremely dangerous job, with a fatality rate more than 20 times higher than other professions. Sadly, over the years, many vessels and crew members have been lost at sea. In 1988 the Seattle Fishermen's Memorial was created at the terminal, between docks 7 and 8, to honor those fishermen and fisherwomen who have perished at sea.

Designed by Seattle sculptor Ron Petty, the solemn sculpture features a heroic fisherman standing on top of a column, hauling in a fish. It looks like a halibut, but Petty says in a written description of the memorial that this is a composite fish of black cod, salmon, herring, various rock fish, and other species. At the base of the column is a band of life-sized bronze fish and shellfish. And flanking the column are two low granite walls with bronze plates inscribed with the names of local commercial fishers who have been lost. The list of more than 675 names begins in 1900, with space for new names to be added.

Often, no bodies are retrieved from accidents at sea, and the memorial serves as a stand-in for gravesites. When you visit, you may see flowers, laminated photos, handwritten notes, candles, stuffed animals, and other tokens of remembrance left by friends, family members and, in some cases, strangers. An annual dedication is held each year on the first Sunday in May.

Address 3919 18th Avenue W, Seattle, WA 98119, www.seattlefishermensmemorial.org, info@seattlefishermensmemorial.org | **Getting there** Bus 31 to W Emerson Place & 21st Avenue W | **Hours** Unrestricted | **Tip** Fishermen's Terminal has three restaurants: Chinook's At Salmon Bay, Little Chinooks, Bay Cafe, Highliner Public House, and the Wild Salmon Seafood Market (3919 18th Avenue W, www.portseattle.org/maritime/fishermen-terminal).

35 Former Ford Factory

Model T's moved along a multi-story assembly line

Thousands of cars of all makes and models stream by the Public Storage building at a busy intersection in South Lake Union each day. Customers stop there to visit their self-storage units. But between March 1914 and January 1932, this 5-story reinforced concrete building with brick veneer and lots of glass was an assembly plant for the Ford Motor Company.

Henry Ford had traveled to Seattle in 1909 to welcome the winners of a transcontinental auto race his company was sponsoring as part of the Alaska Yukon Pacific Exposition, Seattle's first World's Fair. A Ford Model T that made the trip from New York in 23 days was disqualified for a rules violation after having been declared the race winner. But Ford did not hold that against the city. A few years later, when the American industrialist was looking to expand Model T production beyond Michigan, Seattle's proximity to a rail shipping hub and a port "made the city a perfect location for the first automotive plant on the West Coast," says Renee Crist, Curator of Collections at LeMay-America's Car Museum in Tacoma.

Model T automobiles built at Ford's South Lake Union plant started with components sent by rail from Michigan. Car frames would begin their journey on an assembly line that started on the building's top floor and then move by conveyor to the ground floor, with workers adding parts along the way. Thousands of cars were produced in this plant each year, with demand eventually outstripping the plant's capacity. In 1932, Ford moved production to a much larger assembly plant with an onsite showroom at 4735 E Marginal Way in the industrial area of South Seattle. Unfortunately, that sprawling, more modern, one-story facility (now on the National Register of Historic Places) was shuttered after just six months because the Great Depression was putting a very serious dent in car sales nationwide.

Address 700 Fairview Avenue N, Seattle, WA 98109 | Getting there Bus C to Fairview Avenue N & Valley Street | Hours Unrestricted from the outside only | Tip The nearby South Lake Union branch of Flatstick Pub, with miniature golf and beers galore, is on the spot where William O. McKay once operated an opulent Ford car dealership (609 Westlake Avenue N, www.flatstickpub.com).

36 Geocaching Headquarters
Mecca for modern treasure hunters

The outdoor treasure hunting game of geocaching challenges participants to use Global Positioning System (GPS) coordinates, puzzle-solving skills, and enthusiasm for adventure to find hidden containers known as geocaches in locations around the world. The pastime traces its modern roots to May 3, 2000, just a day after the US government gave the public access to satellite technology that makes it possible for anyone (not just the US Department of Defense) to pinpoint their exact location on Earth. One creative GPS enthusiast hid a bucket containing a logbook and some trinkets in the woods near Portland, OR and challenged others to find it using only GPS coordinates. Anyone who located the container was asked to sign the logbook and "Take some stuff, leave some stuff." Today, geocaching is a popular sport with more than 3.2 million active geocaches tucked away in every country, except North Korea.

For geocachers, a stop at Geocaching HQ in Seattle's Fremont neighborhood is a bucket list destination. The company's Visitor Center documents the hobby's history and growth, offers a variety of interactive activities, and is filled with geocaching treasures – some are hidden, but most are in plain sight. You'll be able to locate the HQ Geocache, which many consider a milestone find.

You'll also find a free photo booth – take one strip with you; leave one there for the album – a live map constantly updated with the latest geocache finds, notable geocoins, and a display of 50 rare trackables, which are the game pieces players move around the world. See if you can spot memorabilia that includes two trackables that went to the International Space Station. You can shop for gear and game souvenirs, and self-guided tours are free. Drop-ins are welcome, but during summer and busy seasons, it's best to RSVP on the website to let them know you plan to visit.

Address 837 N 34th Street, Suite 300, Seattle, WA 98103, www.geocachinghq.com, hqvisits@geocaching.com | **Getting there** Bus 31, 32, 40, 62 to Fremont Avenue N & N 34th Street | **Hours** Mon–Fri 9:30am–noon & 1–4:30pm, reservations required | **Tip** Download a HG GeoTour passport to explore Fremont, the self-proclaimed "Center of the Universe," with stops at Gas Works Park, the Fremont Troll, and six other locations (www.geocaching.com/play/geotours/hq).

37 __ Georgetown Steam Plant

Engineering marvel and electrical time machine

Don't worry if you know little of steam turbines, reinforced concrete, or early 20th-century Seattle history. You'll learn about all that when visiting the 1906 Georgetown Steam Plant. And you'll get to hang out around huge, historically significant machinery too.

This steam plant was built in 1906–1907 on 18 acres of land along the Duwamish River, by the Seattle Electric Company, which sought a reliable power source for its electric streetcar system. Overseeing construction was engineer Frank Gilbreth who, with his wife Lillian, pioneered time-motion efficiencies. (The duo was later depicted in the *Cheaper by the Dozen* books and movies.) The plant was supposed to be built of steel and brick. But after the 1906 San Francisco earthquake, Gilbreth called for a seismically stronger and more fire-resistant concrete reinforced structure instead, making this plant one of the first major buildings on the West Coast built this way.

Upstairs in the T-shaped building is a giant boiler room, where coal and oil were burned. Below, the sprawling engine room contains two of the only Curtis Vertical Steam Turbines left in place in the world. A smaller, more efficient horizontal turbine added in 1919 is here too. As impressive as the plant was, "Its usefulness was short lived because steam power was replaced by hydropower," says Julianna Ross of Seattle City Light, the city utility that operated the plant from 1951 until its decommissioning in the late 1970s.

Saved from the wrecking ball due to its historical significance, the plant now hosts monthly open houses where longtime volunteers are on hand to explain exactly how the machinery works. As a bonus, there is often live music. In the past, a few cultural events were staged in the building as well. Going forward, a partnership with a local non-profit will turn the site into a museum and cultural center.

Address 6605 13th Avenue S, Seattle, WA 98108, +1 (206) 763-2542, www.georgetownsteamplant.org | Getting there Bus 60, 107 to S Albro Place & Stanley Avenue S | Hours Monthly second Sat 10am–2pm | Tip The nearby Mini Mart City Park is a pocket park and art center on the site of a former gas station (6525 Ellis Avenue S, www.minimartcitypark.com).

38__Georgetown Trailer Park Mall

A hip place to shop, snack, or get hitched

As malls go, the Georgetown Trailer Park Mall is odd but charming. Eight vintage trailers house stylish and carefully curated local businesses that sell everything from vintage clothing, jewelry, and funky home décor to hand-crafted art, crafts, accessories, baked goods and more. Badder Body, for example, offers skincare products made of natural vegan-organic ingredients. The Royal Mansion Gallery, named after the 1951 Spartan Royal Mansion Travel Trailer it is housed in, displays work by more than 40 area artists.

Mall owner Mary Enslow says it's all a great fit for the historic, industrial Georgetown neighborhood. Even the very low-flying planes going to or from nearby Boeing Field and SeaTac Airport add to the charm (see ch. 9). "The planes can be loud and are close enough that it's exciting when they roar by," says Enslow, "Especially for kids."

Noise from airplanes and passing trains is often the backdrop for ceremonies taking place in the converted shipping container that is home to easy and stress-free Shotgun Ceremonies Wedding Chapel. "Many couples don't like big production weddings. Some need to get married because of visa issues, medical insurance, military benefits, etc. And some have families that would make a big wedding complicated. So they come here instead," says chapel owner and officiant Bronwen Stevenson. "Others just want a quirky, non-traditional vibe or a Vegas-style elopement with an Elvis impersonator, which we can provide."

Stevenson notes that the trailer park mall offers couples everything needed for a wedding. In addition to the chapel's outdoor gazebo and dressing room in a trailer, the adjacent Star Brass Lounge hosts receptions. Rooms above the Georgetown Arts & Cultural Center are available for overnight stays.

Address 5805 Airport Way S, Seattle, WA 98108, www.georgetowntrailerparkmall.com, gttrailerparkmall@gmail.com | Getting there Bus 125 to Airport Way S & S Doris Street | Hours Sat 11am–6pm (open later during Art Attack every second Sat), Sun 11am–4pm | Tip Enjoy a tour and a tasting at Georgetown Brewing Company (5200 Denver Avenue S, www.georgetownbeer.com).

39__Gessner Mansion

A gambler's haunted home

Seattle's Georgetown neighborhood is a fun and funky, blue-collar arts and light industrial community with warehouses, pubs, artist studios, coffeeshops, and the odd 'bonus' of low flying planes making their approach to nearby Boeing Field (see ch. 9). Georgetown's housing is eclectic too, leaning to modest bungalows, old brick apartment buildings, and a smattering of modern townhouses. That is just one reason the peach-colored, 3-story, Queen Anne-style house with the wraparound porch and black iron fence stands out. Another reason: the house is said to be haunted.

Known as the Gessner Mansion, or the Georgetown Castle, this turreted house was built in 1902 by Peter Gessner, well-known in town as a gambler and blackjack dealer. Gessner planned to live there with his wife, Anna Elizabeth (Lizzie), but she took up with the manager of the poultry and rabbit farm the couple owned. So Gessner moved in on his own. A year later, he was dead. The coroner said Gessner committed suicide by drinking carbolic acid. Others believed it was murder.

Lizzie and her new husband (the farm manager) lived in the house for a few years. Over time, the sprawling space has served as home to a brothel, a speakeasy, a rooming house, a social club for the local baseball team, and, as it is now, a private residence. But it seems some of the former residents stayed on. Gessner's ghost is said to haunt the second floor. Assorted female spirits thought to be hanging around are tied to a mishmash of gory stories. In one, the ghost is a former brothel worker named Mary Christian, who was strangled by her lover, a magician. In another, the spirit that haunts the house belongs to Sarah, the wife of one of Gessner's sons. When it was discovered that Sarah had become pregnant by another man, local legend has it that her husband killed the baby and buried it under that nice wraparound porch.

Address 6420 Carleton Avenue S, Seattle, WA 98108 | **Getting there** Bus 60, 124 to Corson Avenue S & S Warsaw Street | **Hours** Unrestricted from the outside only | **Tip** Boost your spirits at the Hangar Cafe, known for crepes, waffles, and savory treats too (6261 13th Avenue S, www.thehangarcafe.com).

40 Giant Shoes Peep Show

Footwear to fit giants

When Dan Eskenazi was a kid, he would hang out at his grandfather's shoe repair shop in downtown Seattle and marvel at the giant pair of boots – size 37AA – that were on display in the shop window.

The boots were given to his grandfather in the late 1930s during a promotional tour by Robert Wadlow who, at 8 feet 11.1 inches tall, held the Guinness World Record title for World's Tallest Man. Unfortunately, those boots disappeared when the shoe repair shop closed in the 1960s. But Eskenazi has been searching for them ever since. In fact, a $1,000 reward for their return is still outstanding. While chasing down that childhood memory, Eskenazi began collecting antique oversized shoes. "Many were advertising tools and novelty items," says Eskenazi. "And for a while they were all in my living room." Today a selection of those big shoes can be seen at Seattle's Pike Place Market in a lively wall exhibit promoted, in circus sideshow graphics, as the "World Famous Giant Shoe Museum." Shoes are displayed peepshow like, behind curtained windows and brass eyepieces, or in shadows. Quarters open curtains or turn on lights so viewers may gaze in wonder at the treasures inside.

On a rotating platter in one window is a single shoe once worn by Wadlow, with his name stamped inside. In another window is a 150-pound, 5-foot-long leather shoe from the 1920s dubbed "The Colossus" and labeled "The Largest Wingtip in Captivity." For a few quarters more viewers can open other curtained windows to see an outlandishly large clown's shoe, a 4-foot-long military boot, and other fun and fabulously large footwear.

While there, be sure to see how you measure up against the life-sized portrait of Robert Wadlow. And look closely at the vintage photographs. In one, you can spot Dan Eskenazi's Uncle Jack at the shoe-repair store wearing Robert Wadlow's missing boots.

Address 1501 Pike Place, Shop No. 424, Pike Place Market, Seattle, WA 98101 | Getting there Bus 1, 2, 3, 4, 7 to 3rd Avenue and Pine Street; Light Rail to Westlake (1 Line) | Hours Daily 10am–5pm | Tip The Market Magic Shop, across from the Giant Shoe Museum, is the oldest magic shop in the Pacific Northwest (1501 Pike Place, Shop No. 427, www.marketmagicshop.com).

41__Grand Illusion

Eclectic films reel out in a quirky space

In 1970, Randy Finley and two partners opened a small cinema, known as "The Movie House," in a cramped space once occupied by a dentist's office. The theater was furnished with old seats and curtains scavenged from other area theaters, "and was so small that Finley hung a sign over the urinal in the men's restroom asking patrons not to flush while a movie was running," according to HistoryLink.org. "It showed offbeat, independent, and foreign films that were much harder to come by in Seattle back then," says Brian Alter, general manager of the now volunteer-run Grand Illusion Cinema, named after French director Jean Renoir's famous anti-war film. It is Seattle's longest running independent film house.

The theater continues to screen a line-up of new indie films, foreign films, "plus any other oddities we can find," says Alter. As it has since the early days, the theater shows the holiday classic, *It's a Wonderful Life*, each December. "Some speculate that those screenings sparked a reappraisal of the film that led to its enduring popularity from the late 70s until present days," says Alter.

Over the years, the theater has hosted movie fans, film fanatics, and some well-known visitors. Filmmaker Quentin Tarantino held a secret screening at the theater in 2001 during the Seattle International Film Festival, and award-winning animator Don Hertzfeldt (*It's Such a Beautiful Day*) "was so intrigued by a trap door in our projection booth that leads outside that he wanted to exit the cinema through it," says Alter.

Posters in the theater's lobby pay tribute to past film series, such as "Festival of Depression" and the "Blob-a-thon," a sci-fi celebration of all three oozy movies starring The Blob. The red-curtain-lined auditorium hosts 70 worn seats covered in velvety floral fabric. And it is now fine to flush to the toilet in the men's restroom during a movie.

Address 1403 NE 50th Street, Seattle, WA 98105, +1 (206) 523-3935, www.grandillusioncinema.org, info@grandillusioncinema.org | **Getting there** Bus 79 to NE 50th Street & University Way NE | **Hours** See website for schedule | **Tip** The Blue Moon, an iconic dive bar in the University District, opened in 1934, right after prohibition ended (712 NE 45th Street, www.thebluemoonseattle.com).

42___Granite Curling Club

Not just shuffleboard on ice

Curling competitions are broadcast on TV every four years during the Olympic Winter Games. And soon after, Seattle's Granite Curling Club gets calls from people wondering what all that sweeping, yelling, and sliding of big stones across the ice is all about. "It definitely heightens awareness," says club spokesman Tom FitzGerald about the sport that traces its roots back to 16th-century Scotland and a game that involved sliding giant stones over the rough surfaces of frozen ponds. Over many years, the game made its way to other cold climates, including the Netherlands, Canada, and the United States, and today it is played indoors, where temperature and ice conditions are carefully controlled.

Seattle's Granite Curling Club (named for the rock used to make the game's curling stones, or rocks, that weigh approximately 42 pounds each) opened in 1961 with five iced playing surfaces, known as sheets, each about 150 feet long and about 14 feet wide. Now the largest and oldest curling facility on the West Coast, the club boasts of being home to more national champions curlers than any other club in the United States.

While it may look like shuffleboard on ice, curling seems more complicated – and fun. It is played with two teams of four players, who each send two stones down the sheet towards a target, or 'house.' As the stones glide, players sweep the path with special brooms to keep the stones moving smoothly and on course. There is a bit more to it, of course. The curling curious are welcome to ask questions and watch curlers of all ages and abilities from the warm, dry viewing area above the club's ice sheets, for free, during league nights, which are usually Monday–Friday evenings from late October through April. For a hands-on experience, the club also hosts 90-minute open house events where you can learn curling basics and play a short game.

Address 1440 N 128th Street, Seattle, WA 98133, +1 (206) 362-2446, www.curlingseattle.org, curling@curlingseattle.org | **Getting there** Bus 345 to N 130th Street & Ashworth Avenue N | **Hours** See website | **Tip** Skate on the same ice as Seattle's NHL team, The Kraken, when the Iceplex, their practice rink, opens for public skate sessions during lunch hours, evenings, and on weekends (10601 5th Avenue NE, www.krakencommunityiceplex.com).

43 __ Great Wheel

Great spot for a spin or a proposal

Ferris wheels, also known as observation wheels, were once found only at amusement parks and summer fairs. Today, you will spot them in an increasing number of urban settings, including the Seattle waterfront. This one is not the country's tallest Ferris wheel, but from its perch on the end of Pier 57, the 175-foot-tall Seattle Great Wheel, built in 2012, still lays claims to being the tallest Ferris wheel on the Pacific Coast.

That is one just reason to board one of the wheel's 42 enclosed, climate-controlled gondolas. A better reason? The unbeatable views. The wheel extends about 40 feet beyond the end of the pier, and during a standard, three-revolution ride (and weather permitting), you can see the Space Needle, downtown sports stadiums, the city skyline, West Seattle, the Cascade Mountains, and boat traffic galore in Elliott Bay. "It's right by my office, and I've ridden it thousands of times," says Troy Griffith, whose family owns the Great Wheel and several other Miners Landing attractions, "And I'm always blown away by those views."

Each gondola holds up to eight riders. If you want to ride alone, impress a date, make a memorable marriage proposal, or mark a special occasion, request the private VIP Cabin #42. It holds four people and cannot be reserved ahead of time. But if you pay the extra fee, you go to the front of the line and ride in the glass-bottomed gondola with leather seats, a sound system, bonus rotations, photos, cocktails, and souvenir t-shirts.

If you'd rather stay on the ground, keep in mind that the wheel is covered in more than 500,000 LED lights. So, you can swing by any evening to enjoy the structure lit up in never-ending patterns and color combinations. Light shows often mark holidays or celebrate local sports teams, but custom light shows for gender reveals and other special events can be arranged.

Address Pier 57 – Miners Landing, 1301 Alaskan Way, Seattle, WA 98101, +1 (206) 623-8607, www.seattlegreatwheel.com, greatwheel@pier57seattle.com | Getting there Bus 1, 2 to 2nd Avenue & Pike Street; Light Rail to University Street (1 Line) | Hours Daily 11am – 9pm | Tip For great views at ground level, walk along Alaskan Way, stopping at Waterfront Park, Pier 62, and the Seattle Art Museum's Olympic Sculpture Park (2901 Western Avenue, www.seattleartmuseum.org).

44__ Greenest Office Building

Six floors of eco-goodness and sustainability

Seattle's Bullitt Foundation wanted office space to reflect the environmental philanthropy's mission of safeguarding the natural environment. To that end, it commissioned an experimental structure that would incorporate as many energy saving systems and eco-friendly materials as possible and mimic the behavior of a Douglas-fir forest. The plan worked. When it opened in 2013, the six-story, 50,000-square-foot Bullitt Center on Seattle's Capitol Hill became the "world's greenest office building."

A rooftop system of 575 solar panels powers the building. Rainfall is harvested and stored in cisterns that supply all needed water. Radiant floors fed by 26 geothermal wells 400 feet below the site provide heat. Greywater from sinks and showers is cleaned and put back into the aquifer. And a weather station hooked up to a computer tells an external venetian blind system when to raise, lower, or tilt so just the right amount of light hits the building's high-efficiency windows. "It's like a living organism and one of my favorite building features," says Denis Hayes, the Bullitt Foundation's president and CEO, and coordinator of the first Earth Day back in 1970. The building has parking for bicycles, but none for cars. An energy-collecting elevator is tucked away, in favor of an 'irresistible stairway,' a term Hayes coined, that encourages exercise and tenant interactions.

Until recently, the Bullitt Center also had waterless toilets feeding basement composters that made fertilizer from human waste. Due to system design problems, the building switched to vacuum flush toilets connected to the sewer system. "I'm sad about the toilets," said Hayes, "But I think of the building as a combination of 40 or 50 science fair experiments that were all testing bleeding edge technology. If none of them had failed, we might have been accused of not being daring enough."

Address 1501 E Madison Street, Seattle, WA 98122, www.bullittcenter.org, info@bullitt.org | Getting there Bus 12 to E Madison Street & 15th Avenue | Hours Tours offered Tue 4pm & Sat noon | Tip The Hanukkah song "I Have a Little Dreidel" was composed and written by Samuel Goldfarb while working as the music director of the Reform Jewish temple across the street. Temple de Hirsch Sinai (1511 E Pike Street, www.templedehirschsinai.org).

45 Green Lake Murder Site

Enjoy your picnic, but remember Sylvia

Seattle's Green Lake Park is one of the most popular and pleasant recreation sites in the city. Designed by the Olmsted Brothers Firm between 1907 and 1912, the park is an urban oasis of trees, plants, birds, and waterfowl. It offers facilities for swimming, boating, playing sports, picnicking, or attending theater in a converted bathhouse. On sunny days, the 2.8-mile path encircling the 259-acre lake teems with people running, walking, skating, and biking.

Just off that path, on the north end of the park between the wading pool and the boathouse, is Gaines Point. With benches and a picnic table, it is a lovely spot to stop for a rest. But back in the 1920s, this was the site of a brutal and sensational murder.

On the morning of June 17, 1926, a pair of women's shoes and then the nearly naked body of 22-year-old Sylvia Gaines were discovered near the water. Police determined that she had been murdered the night before by being choked and hit on the head with the bloody rock found nearby. The prime suspect: her father, Wallace C. "Bob" Gaines.

During a scandalous trial, the public learned that Sylvia's parents had split when she was five. In 1925, after graduating from Smith College, Sylvia came to Seattle and moved in with her dad and his second wife. The motive for murder, the prosecution claimed, was that after months of an incestuous relationship between father and daughter, Sylvia was determined to leave. After a quarrel, her father followed Sylvia to Green Lake and killed her in a jealous, alcohol-induced rage that he tried to make look like a random sexual attack by tearing her clothes and dragging the body. Bob Gaines was found guilty and hanged for the crime in Walla Walla on August 31, 1928. Sylvia's cremated ashes were sent to her mother in Massachusetts. And the unmarked point of land on Green Lake was dubbed Gaines Point in Sylvia's honor.

Address v7201 E Green Lake Drive N, Seattle, WA 98115, www.seattle.gov/parks/find/parks/green-lake-park | Getting there Bus to 45 E Greenlake Drive N & Meridian Avenue N | Hours Unrestricted | Tip On a more pleasant note, the two benches at Gaines Point are in memory of Florence and Harry McIntyre. The plaques give their birth and death dates (Harry lived to be 100) but neglect to mention that the couple was married for 50 years.

46 __ Greenwood Pencil Box

Supplies for creativity that support good causes

Sometimes you just need the right tools, some words of encouragement, and the physical and emotional space to make progress on a
creative project. The Greenwood Pencil Box is a good place to start.
This shop entices passersby inside with an interactive Story Wall, a
3D street sign evoking the tip of a sharpened pencil, and plenty of
gear and attire to help get creative minds in motion.

The offerings here lean towards the unusual and the locally made.
Items are chosen for their ability to spark imagination, be meaning-
ful, be recrafted, or be used for writing or making art. The shelves
are filled with everything from candles that have the scent of places
in the Pacific Northwest, to puzzles, games, journals, notepads, and
books on writing and the creative process. The writing instruments
here include every color of fine-tipped art pen and, of course, a wide
assortment of pencils, pencil sharpeners, and erasers that are beautiful to hold and use.

Proceeds from the shop fuel the work of two local non-profits:
The Greater Seattle Bureau of Fearless Ideas and Sanctuary Art
Center. Both groups offer free creative learning programs for area
youth and young adults. Beyond shopping for writing and art supplies, the public can support the organizations and get a taste for
their activities during live, in-store readings and performances.
There is also that inviting Story Wall in the front window where
anyone may sit down and add a few lines to an ongoing series of
collectively written stories being typed out on a vintage, bright red,
IBM Selectric typewriter.

Those who remember when this site was home to the similarly
minded Greenwood Space Supply Co. will be glad to know that the
"Atomic Teleporter" that functioned as a real and metaphorical portal
between the shop and an adjacent classroom is now a 22-foot-tall,
upside down, No. 2 pencil that serves the same purpose.

Address 8414 Greenwood Avenue N, Seattle, WA 98103, +1 (206) 725-2625, www.greenwoodpencilbox.com, store@greenwoodpencilbox.com | Getting there Bus 45 to Greenwood Avenue N & N 85th Street | Hours Tue–Thu noon–6pm, Fri & Sat noon–7pm | Tip Seattle ReCreative down the street is filled with donated surplus goods yearning to become art (8408 Greenwood Avenue N, www.seattlerecreative.org).

47 Grossology Bathrooms
Lessons in the loos

Discovery, technology, education disguised as fun – the Pacific Science Center has it all.

IMAX movies? Check – there are two state-of-the-art theaters. Laser shows? Check – at almost 80 feet in diameter, the Laser Dome is the largest and longest operating domed laser theater in the world. History? Check – the building was the US Science Pavilion during the 1962 World's Fair and was designed by Minoru Yamasaki, who was also the architect of New York City's World Trade Center.

But when it is time to 'go,' we head for the Grossology-themed restrooms beneath the Paccar IMAX theater. In both loos, colorful and cartoony wall treatments explain, "If you eat a lot of beets, your pee will actually be colored red." And also, "There are people all over the world who drink pee because they believe it is healthy. Fresh urine is cleaner than poop, spit, or the skin on your face, because healthy pee is not home to bacteria." An illustration entitled, "Poo Pinching," shows the body's waste path and gives a detailed explanation of the connection between peristalsis and a successful poo. Another shows a naked king sitting on a toilet. The explanation? "In France during the 1600s, it was considered a great honor to speak to King Louis XIV while he relieved himself on his not-so-kingly throne."

The toilet tidbits are souvenirs from past exhibits based on the *Grossology* books by the author/illustrator team Sylvia Branzei and Jack Keely. The books are filled with accurate and amusing explanations of farting, belching, pooping, and other bodily functions that are perfectly normal, but not often publicly discussed. "It's all the things that kids giggle and talk about amongst themselves," says Diana Johns, the Pacific Science Center's Vice President of Exhibits & Life Sciences. "And they go nuts when they see it just out there in the bathroom like that."

Address 200 2nd Avenue N, Seattle, WA 98109, +1 (206) 443-2001, www.pacificsciencecenter.org, gs@pacsci.org | **Getting there** Seattle Center Monorail to Seattle Center; bus 1, 2, 8, 13 to Denny Way & 2nd Avenue N | **Hours** Wed–Sun 10am–5pm | **Tip** The Seattle Children's Theatre is next door on the Seattle Center Campus (201 Thomas Street, www.sct.org).

48 Hat 'n' Boots

A supersized howdy for visitors to Oxbow Park

Seattle's claim to being the site of the world's first gas station in 1907 has been challenged, but you'll be hard pressed to find anyone who will dispute the fact that the city once had the *coolest* gas station.

The Hat 'n' Boots Tex Gas Station that Buford Seals opened on Highway 99 near Seattle's Georgetown neighborhood in 1954 was impossible to ignore. The station office was housed inside a giant red cowboy hat that was 19 feet tall and 44 feet in diameter. The restrooms were inside a pair of 22-foot-tall cowboy boots beside the hat. Out front were nine pump islands.

The Western-themed gas station was both an attraction and a success. For several years, it was the state's most profitable place to fill 'er up. And the station's fame grew when word got out that Elvis Presley had pulled into the station to fill up the tank of his Cadillac. The story could be true: Elvis was in town during the 1962 Seattle World's Fair to film the movie *It Happened at the World's Fair*, and he did take a road trip while here.

Buford Seals had plans to build a grand Frontier Village shopping complex near the gas station, but that never happened. In the early 1960s, Interstate 5 was built, and traffic was diverted away from Highway 99 and the station. Sadly, the Hat 'n' Boots shut down, and the eye-catching site began to fade and rust. In 1997 it was slated for demolition. But that's when local artists, Georgetown residents, and fans of roadside attractions came riding to the rescue. Protests took place. Grants applications were written. Money was raised. And the Hat 'n' Boots was declared a city landmark, which cleared the way for the structures to be moved, repaired, restored, and repainted.

Now the Hat 'n' Boots are impossible to ignore at Oxbow Park in Georgetown. You cannot fill up your tank or use the boots as a loo, but you might see people picnicking under the cowboy hat brim.

Address 6430 Corson Avenue S, Seattle, WA 98108, www.seattle.gov/parks/find/parks/oxbow-park | Getting there Bus 60, 124 Corson Avenue S & S Warsaw Street | Hours Daily 4am – 11:30pm | Tip Georgetown is home to the Fran's Chocolates flagship shop and factory, where you can see how the handcrafted confections are made (5900 Airport Way S, www.frans.com).

49__Hot Tub Boats
Rub-a-dub-dub, tour the lake in a tub

There are many ways to experience Lake Union, the 580-acre freshwater lake within the Seattle city limits. Fly over it in a Kenmore Air seaplane tour. Gaze out at it from numerous restaurants, bars, and parks on shore. Or you can get out on the water in kayaks, paddle boards, canoes, rowboats, electric boats, sailboats, and yachts. Visitors and locals alike can see all the inspiring views from sightseeing cruises offered by Argosy, Emerald City Pirates, and Seattle Water Tours, which runs popular ice cream cruises.

One of the more unusual ways to tour Lake Union, though, is in a vessel that is officially neither a boat nor a hot tub, but a "hot tub boat" that has been carefully and, according to a company spokesman, 'magically' engineered for buoyancy. Built by hand by shipwrights in Ballard, each fiberglass boat has classic teak decking, a hot tub insert, and an electric motor that you can maneuver from inside the tub with a joystick to a safe and leisurely maximum speed of 5 mph.

A small, diesel-fired boiler on board keeps the temperature of the tub's 2,500 pounds of water heated to 104 degrees Fahrenheit, the maximum temperature allowed. Tubs hold up to six people, and they are drained and sanitized after each use. They have dry storage too. Maps pointing out the best spots to see the Space Needle, Gas Works Park, historic boats, and, yes, the *Sleepless in Seattle* houseboat, are included. Food and drinks are allowed on board; alcohol and nudity are not.

These boats first hit Lake Union waters back in 2012, the brainchild of Adam Karpenske, a wooden boat shipwright by trade, who was living on a local houseboat and craving the convenience of a home hot tub. Instead of chopping up his boat, he worked out the unusual and innovative design for hot tub boats, which are now popular for small group outings, proposals, and one wedding so far.

Address 2520 Westlake Avenue N, Seattle, WA 98109, +1 (206) 771-9883, www.hottubboats.com, info@hottubboats.com | **Getting there** Bus 40 to Westlake Avenue N & Westlake Avenue N | **Hours** Daily 8am – 11pm | **Tip** Seattle Donut Boat Co. rents brightly colored, circular donut-shaped boats equipped with umbrellas, round picnic tables, and small electric motors steered by tillers (1001 Fairview Avenue N, www.seattledonutboat.com).

50 Howe Street Stairs

Seattle's longest staircase is quite a workout

Seattle's hilly topography plays host to more than 650 sets of public stairs. Many are utilitarian shortcuts from here to there. Some go nowhere. Others zigzag creatively up and down hillsides offering surprising views, challenging workouts, and glimpses of grand homes, cool art, and quirky gardens. At least one is said to be haunted (see ch. 104). And many were built more than a century ago as part of a network of neighborhood footpaths that also helped early commuters access trolley stops.

The Howe Street Stairway punches the stairway ticket on a variety of these points. Built in 1911 with 388 concrete steps and spanning an elevation of 160 feet, this stairway was originally built as a link between two streetcar lines and is now Seattle's longest stairway. "Their length and age are just part of their inherent charm," explain Cathy and Jake Jaramillo, authors of *Seattle Stairway Walks: An Up-and-Down Guide to the City Neighborhood*. "But the Howe Street Stairs also make a durable connection between two quite different neighborhoods separated by Interstate 5, by a large difference in elevation and by completely different land uses."

At the bottom of the stairs is the Eastlake neighborhood, an industrial/commercial hub on the Lake Union shore. At the top is Capitol Hill, a residential area, home to grand 1900s-era residences on "Millionaires Row," and the historic Olmsted Brothers designed Volunteer Park (see ch. 101). In between, on 13 sets of stairs, is what the Jaramillos describe as a "scenic byway," providing views of several shoreline street-ends and the six-mile multi-use path around Lake Union known as the Cheshiahud Trail. The stairs offer a challenging workout and will take you under the freeway and past the I-5 Colonnade, which was the nation's first urban mountain bike skills park, designed with areas for novice, intermediate, and advanced riders.

Address 810 E Howe Street, Seattle, WA 98102 | Getting there Bus 49 to 10th Avenue & E Howe Street | Hours Unrestricted | Tip Blaine Staircase, Seattle's second longest staircase at 293 steps, parallels Howe Street Stairs to the South (10th Avenue E and E Blaine Street). Be sure to stop at Streissguth Gardens as you climb.

51 International Fountain

Seattle Center's water feature has its own DJ

When it debuted at the space age-themed 1962 Seattle World's Fair, the International Fountain had spikey water nozzles on a silver metal dome and a surrounding field of jagged white "moon" rocks. A makeover in 1995 by WET Design (creators of the Bellagio Hotel's dancing fountains in Las Vegas) made the fountain far more playful and welcoming. Today, it has colored lights and hundreds of flat jets, including 56 micro shooters and 4 super shooters that can send recycled water more than 120 feet high.

One of five 'Big Show' water programs choreographed to music erupts every half hour, with Duke Ellington, Aaron Copeland's *Billy the Kid*, Beethoven's *9th Symphony*, and a mashup of NW rock 'n' roll legends in the mix. Between the 12-minute shows, the fountain flows in a pleasant fleur-de-lis pattern to locally crafted soundtrack. For 26 years, until late 2022, it was local musician and DJ James Whetzel refreshing the two to three-hour mixes every two weeks. "Machines under the fountain run the programs. One for the 'big shows' and one for my mixes," says Whetzel, "I used to burn CDs for the 100-disc CD player down there, but now it all goes on a sound card."

The fountain programs also play in the Armory, Seattle Center's indoor food and event venue. They are more energetic during warmer months and become mellower in fall and winter. "I'd try to create an environment that lets you interact with the water, but also talk, dance, and listen. It's like an art installation that becomes a soundtrack for the fountain," he says. An ethnomusicologist, Whetzel also made his mixes culturally inclusive and welcoming for all ages. And he made a point of including new music and work by local artists. The new DJ, when chosen, will surely do the same.

You and your kids can enjoy splashing in the fountain on warm summer days. When you get home, you can tune into the fountain music mixes at: www.mixcloud.com/InternationalFountain.

Address Seattle Center, 305 Harrison Street, Seattle, WA 98109, +1 (206) 684-7200 | Getting there Seattle Monorail to Seattle Center; bus 1, 2, 8, 13 to 1st Avenue N & Republican Street | Hours Unrestricted | Tip Music and sound are key elements in Seattle Center's all-ages Artists at Play playground near the Museum of Pop Culture (www.seattlecenter.com/explore/attractions/artists-at-play).

52 Ivar's Salmon House
Spot the oosiks

The best cities have one: a quirky character whose odd actions are woven into local history. In Seattle, Ivar Haglund owns that title.

In 1938, Haglund opened a downtown aquarium on Pier 54 with a fish & chips stand that grew into a regional restaurant chain. He coined the "Keep Clam" motto and was a whiz with advertising stunts and pranks. When a railroad tank car spilled thousands of gallons of syrup on the tracks near Pier 54, Haglund rushed over with a giant spoon and a pile of pancakes. He staged a wrestling match between an octopus and a prize fighter. He hosted clam-eating contests and once took his seal, Patsy, for a walk through a department store to visit Santa. You get the picture. To Haglund's delight, local news outlets got it too.

Ivar's Salmon House, which Haglund built as a cedar replica of a Northwest Native American longhouse, opened on Lake Union's Portage Bay in 1970. It is now an iconic destination as much for the alder-smoked salmon and other dishes as it is for its sail-up and barge dining, and the décor. The exterior and interior are covered in Northwest Native art created and carved by noted artists from the region. Historical photos, art, and artifacts are everywhere, so don't be shy about taking some time before or after your meal to look around. The front door is a 14-foot-high carving of a whale head with its mouth open – the snout forms an awning. In the lobby, a carved "Welcoming Man" stands almost seven feet tall. Four hand-carved Native American canoes hang from the rafters. One is from 1916, and another is from 1929 and 52-feet long. In the Whalemaker Lounge are a pair of whale oosiks, or penis bones. They are, as you may imagine, quite long, but you'll have to squint to see them nestled in with the liquor. Ask your server to point out the houseboat across the water that starred in *Sleepless in Seattle*.

Address 401 NE Northlake Way, Seattle, WA 98105, +1 (206) 632- 0767, www.ivars.com/
salmon-house | Getting there Bus 31, 32 to N 40th Street & 1st Avenue NE | Hours
Sun–Thu 11:30am–8pm, Fri & Sat 11:30am–9pm | Tip A path just west of the Salmon
House leads to Waterway 15, a small park with water access, seating, and views of Lake
Union and the downtown skyline. Look for historic photos on the rocks (4th Avenue NE
and NE Northlake Way).

53 Jimi Hendrix Gravesite

The rock icon's final resting place

The world remembers James Marshall 'Jimi' Hendrix as a pioneering musician and one of the most innovative guitarists of all time. The groundbreaking rock 'n' roll icon is forever linked with Seattle because he was born and raised here, learned to play guitar here, and performed here both before and after he was famous. After his death in 1970 at the age of 27, he was buried in a cemetery in nearby Renton.

By far the most visited Hendrix-related site is his gravesite in Renton's Greenwood Memorial Park. Hendrix's grave was originally marked with a simple, low headstone bearing an etched Stratocaster and the words, "Forever in our Hearts." But in 2002, Hendrix's remains and the headstone were moved to an elaborate, domed, granite gazebo that incorporates a large bronze guitar. Portraits of Hendrix and lyrics to several of his songs in his handwriting are etched onto the inside panels of the memorial's pillars.

A steady stream of rock fans come by to pay their respect to Hendrix, often leaving behind gifts and trinkets that include guitar picks, coins, flowers, bandanas, joints, and, on the etched portraits, many lipstick kisses. You can find this poignant Hendrix memorial in a roundabout on the west side of the cemetery, near the funeral home.

Various spots in the city pay tribute to Hendrix's memory. There is a bronze bust at Garfield High School, a worn plaque on a rock at the Woodland Park Zoo, and a life-sized bronze statue of him on Capitol Hill (1604 Broadway) by artist Daryl Smith, officially titled *The Electric Lady Studio Guitar*, depicting Hendrix playing a Stratocaster. The 2.5-acre Jimi Hendrix Park (Central District, 2400 S Massachusetts Street), next to the Northwest African American Museum, features a stairway adorned with Hendrix's signature and a 105-foot-long, purple metal sculpture with Hendrix's face engraved on it.

Address Greenwood Memorial Park Cemetery, 350 Monroe Avenue NE, Renton, WA 98056, +1 (425) 255-1511, www.jimihendrixmemorial.com | **Getting there** By car, take I-90 East and I-405 S to Exit 4 in Renton | **Hours** Unrestricted | **Tip** Hendrix's dad bought his son's first guitar at Myer's Music, which once stood at 1214 1st Avenue.

54 J. P. Patches Statue

Celebrating Seattle's favorite clowns

You need not have grown up in Seattle to love the wacky exuberance of the life-sized statue on Fremont's Solstice Plaza of two clownish figures, arms locked and running in opposite directions. But it helps if you know some history of the long-running local children's show *The J. P. Patches Show*.

The goofy, mostly unscripted show starred Chris Wedes as red-nosed clown Julius Pierpont Patches (J.P. for short) and sidekick Bob Newman, who played Gertrude, the City Dump telephone operator, plus more than a dozen other characters. Young fans of the show could be a "Patches Pal" by promising to follow wholesome rules, such as "Mind mommy and daddy" and "Share your toys." The KIRO-TV program began airing in 1958 live mornings and afternoons, six days a week for the first 13 years. Later, the show was on mornings only, then just Saturday mornings. The final show aired on September 25, 1981.

Artist Kevin Pettelle watched the show as a kid in Sultan, WA. In 2008, he would be tapped make the bronze sculpture honoring the TV show's stars. "They were idols to me. Like The Beatles," says Pettelle, who spent time with both Wedes and Newman (both now deceased) as the project developed. Beyond capturing the spirit of J. P. Patches and Gertrude, Pettelle added special 'insider' features to the statue. J. P. Patches' cap sports characters from the show, and there's an ICU2-TV frame. Look for the tattoo on Gertrude's arm, a reference to Bob Newman's stint in the Marine Corps. "Be sure to tell people that whatever you do, don't look under Gertrude's skirt," says Pettelle.

The sculpture's official name, *Late for the Interurban*, is a nod to the iconic, often dressed and decorated *Waiting for the Interurban* sculpture by Richard Beyer about 250 feet away, depicting five adults, a kid, and a dog waiting for the electric trolley line that once ran from Seattle to Everett.

Address Solstice Plaza, Fremont Avenue N & N 34th Street, Seattle, WA 98103 | Getting there Bus 31, 32, 40, 62 to Fremont Avenue N & N 34th Street | Hours Unrestricted | Tip The 18-foot-tall Fremont Troll, like the troll in the *Billy Goats Gruff* fairytale, lives under a bridge nearby (N 36th Street and Troll Avenue N under the north end of the Aurora Bridge).

55___KEXP Gathering Space

Watch radio, drink coffee, see a show, buy records

Fans of alternative and indie rock, roots & blues, hip hop, alternative country, and a wide range of other musical genres adore Seattle's KEXP public radio station. The eclectic station broadcasts on-air at 90.3 FM and online and is known worldwide as one of the hippest and most innovative independent stations in the world.

The reputation is well-deserved. In 1988, the station, then KCMU, was the first to give airplay to Nirvana's debut album, *Bleach*, after lead singer and guitarist Kurt Cobain dropped by with a copy. The tradition of debuting work by new artists and welcoming both up-and-coming and established musicians onto the air and into the studios continues today – in a big way.

In 2016, when KEXP moved into new broadcast headquarters at the edge of the Seattle Center campus, the station decided not just to broadcast great sounds out, but to invite the community in. The station hosts hundreds of free live performances each year in its 4,500-square-foot Gathering Space, with a stage and lots of comfortable seating. Garage doors open onto an outdoor courtyard, and there is a viewing window into the broadcast booth. The space also has an art gallery and an espresso bar / café, plus free Wi-Fi. For those who want to take the music home, the radio station has an on-site record shop that is expertly curated by Seattle's Light in the Attic record label, a well-known archival reissue and distribution company. And it's not just music fans who enjoy hanging out at KEXP.

"Musicians really love coming by for live shows," says Rischel Granquist, KEXP's facilities director. "Our engineers make them sound great. We offer an oasis of calm and a place to refresh that includes a green room with a kitchenette, a shower, a washer and dryer, and something else that we've learned musicians really appreciate – a safe place off the street to store their gear."

Address 472 1st Avenue N, Seattle, WA 98109, +1 (206) 520-5800, www.kexp.org/visit, feedback@kexp.org | Getting there Bus D, 1, 2, 8, 13, 32 to Republican Street & 1st Avenue N | Hours See website for hours and events | Tip Indie music fans can also visit Sub Pop, the record and merch shop with locations at the airport and downtown (2130 7th Avenue, www.subop.com).

56 Kirke Park

Resurrected, but not as planned

Today it is a Ballard neighborhood oasis with a hidden nature trail, a sand pit, and a play area with a fun saucer swing set. But for almost 90 years, the site known now as Kirke Park, after the Norwegian word for church, was home to a mysterious, cult-like religious sect. Led by the self-proclaimed prophet Daniel Salwt, the Seventh Elect Church in Israel required its followers to live communally, be vegetarians, give all their possessions and earnings to the church, and practice celibacy. Rumor had, though, that there was a teenage "queen," a handmaiden who shared Salwt's bed.

Many other odd stories swirled through the working-class, Scandinavian neighborhood about the people who lived in the big, dark house hidden from the street by a wall of prickly holly bushes and a high laurel hedge. One that is true is that when Salwt died in 1929, his followers would not let the health department inside to remove the body for three days because they were waiting for their prophet to be resurrected. *The Seattle Times* reported that Salwt's disciples insisted he was "only sleeping" and "gathering strength for the working of a master miracle," even after rigor mortis had begun and a mortician had performed six tests in their presence to prove that Salwt was "just as dead as a man can be."

Church members continued living on the property until well into the late 1980s, when there were reportedly just three or four elderly residents left. City officials eyed the site for a park, but the church would not sell the land until 2008.

Today, the property has been resurrected as a green space with areas for children to enjoy, and a community garden that includes a section where neighbors grow vegetables to donate to area food banks for those in need. To learn more about the history of the site, look for the plaque mounted by the garden on remnants of the sect's unfinished temple foundation.

Address 7028 9th Avenue NW, Seattle, WA 98117, +1 (206) 684-4075 www.seattle.gov/parks/find/parks/kirke-park | Getting there Bus 28 to 8th Avenue NW & NW 70th Street | Hours Daily 4am–11:30pm | Tip Frankie & Jo's, a popular spot for vegan ice cream treats, has a scoop shop nearby with a charming succulent garden out back (1411 NW 70th Street, www.frankieandjos.com).

57 Klondike Gold Rush Park

Seattle struck gold with miners heading north

No, the 80 neatly piled "gold" bars in the front window of the Klondike Gold Rush National Historical Park in Pioneer Square are not real. If they were, they'd weigh a ton and represent just half of the gold that arrived in Seattle with the 68-eight miners aboard the SS *Portland* on July 17, 1897.

Gold had been discovered a year earlier near the Klondike River in Canada's Yukon Territory, and the men disembarking that day had been the first to cash in. Hordes of hopeful miners began rushing north, inspired by reports of "stacks of yellow metal" being unloaded from the steamer and the *Seattle Post-Intelligencer* headline, "Gold! Gold! Gold! Gold!"

Newly minted prospectors could leave from several cities. But thanks to the recent arrival of the railroad and an aggressive promotional campaign, Seattle positioned itself as the "gateway to the gold fields," where gold was said to be "lying on the ground, easy to pick up."

The plan paid off. Of the estimated 100,000 people who sought fortune in the Klondike, 70,000 came through Seattle. And though a scant few miners struck it rich, Seattle's merchants outfitting the miners did just that. "You couldn't enter Canada unless you had a year's worth of provisions, weighing about 2,000 pounds," explains Park Ranger Chris Gibbs. The recommended list included 300 pounds of flour, 150 pounds of bacon, a gross of matches, fur robes, buckets, hatchets, and much more. "Seattle was happy to mine the miners," says Gibbs.

You can learn about the gold rush and its impact on the city at this historical park. Step into the tiny miner's shack and spin the "Wheel of Fortune" to see how rare it was to strike it rich. Or peer at the tiny, portable gold scales that belonged to George Washington Carmack, who, with his First Nations wife and brother-in-law, made the gold field discovery that sparked the Klondike Gold Rush.

Address 319 2nd Avenue S, Seattle, WA 98104, +1 (206) 220-4240, www.nps.gov/klse/index.htm, KLSE_Ranger_Activities@nps.gov | Getting there Light Rail to International District / Chinatown (1 Line); bus 5, 15 to 4th Avenue S & S Jackson Street | Hours See website | Tip Grab a "Trail to Treasure" map for a self-guided, historic walking tour of Pioneer Square. Don't skip the restored grand waiting room of the King Street Station lobby (303 S Jackson Street).

58___KOBO at Higo

An homage to what came before

In the mid-1990s, after living for a while in Japan, Binko Chiong-Bisbee and her husband John Bisbee moved back to Seattle to open KOBO, a small artisan shop and gallery on Capitol Hill that they fill with fine crafts and functional objects sourced from Japan and the Northwest. KOBO at Higo, their second shop and gallery, is in Japantown, part of the historic International District, and is also filled with artist-made treasures. But in this 3,000-square-foot space they also keep alive the spirit and history of the Higo Variety Store, which the Murakami family built and operated as a mainstay of the Japanese community for 75 years.

KOBO opened in the space at the invitation of a Murakami relative. You will see many of the original store's vintage fixtures, glass display cases, and cabinetry now displaying their wares. With items they discovered in the storeroom and help from the Wing Luke Museum (see ch. 106), they created an exhibit area that looks like the original Higo store, complete with glass cases and high shelves stocked with many of the essential items Higo shoppers might have found.

"We wanted people to experience what was there before," says Chiong-Bisbee, "So you can see the adding machine, the cash register, and the typewriter the Murakamis used to run the business. There's also merchandise, such as Japanese toys, sewing notions, dolls, stockings, and canned food items. We even have the large, locally made tins they would have used to store rice crackers."

You can see an interview with Masa and Aya, the sisters (now deceased) who were the last members of the Murakami family to run the Higo store, from your seat at a wooden booth rescued from an old Japantown restaurant. Life-sized, black-and-white photo cutouts of the sisters sit on the exhibit counter. "It's kind of startling to see them," says Chiong-Bisbee. "It's almost like they're there."

Address 604 S Jackson Street, Seattle, WA 98104, +1 (206) 381-3000, www.koboseattle.com, hello@koboseattle.com | Getting there Bus 7, 14, 36 to 5th Avenue S & S Jackson Street; Light Rail to International District/Chinatown (1 Line) | Hours Wed–Sat 11am–5pm | Tip Halfway down Nihonmachi Alley, near KOBO's front door, is Chiyo's Garden, which honors a daughter of the Murakami family who died of tuberculosis in 1937 at age 22 (north side of Jackson Street, between 6th & Maynard Avenues).

59__Kubota Garden

A life, a home, and a garden built and rebuilt

In the Rainier Beach neighborhood in South Seattle, Kubota Garden is a hidden jewel that celebrates the beauty of the Pacific Northwest in a traditional Japanese garden.

The garden was the life's work of Fujitaro Kubota. Born in Japan, he immigrated to the US in 1907 and came to Seattle via San Francisco around 1910. The self-taught nurseryman and horticultural pioneer built a professional garden company. In 1927, he purchased five acres of clear-cut swamp land and then cleared and transformed it into an elaborate series of display gardens, blending Japanese designs with Northwest native plants and materials. Over time, the garden expanded to 20 acres.

Kubota's family lived on the property, but during World War II they were interned with other Japanese families in Idaho's Minidoka prison camp. The family kept the property and rented their home during their absence. But when they returned to Seattle after the war, they had to rebuild their lives – and the gardens.

Kubota continued improving the site, and in 1966, after discriminatory state laws prohibiting Japanese immigrants from owning or leasing land were struck down, he finally became the land's legal owner. The city declared the site a historic landmark in 1981 and, to protect the property from development, acquired the garden in 1987. Today visitors can step through a dramatic, bronze entry gate and wander through gardens, small forests, and hillsides dotted with streams, waterfalls, ponds, rockeries, and Kubota's carefully chosen plantings.

Self-guided tour brochures at the garden entrance and online highlight the trails and point out details about special features, such as the ponds fed by underground springs and Heart Bridge, which resembles a red bridge on Kubota's home island of Shikoku, Japan. The garden is a spiritual and historic contribution by Mr. Kubota for all to enjoy.

Address 9817 55th Avenue S, Seattle, WA 98118, +1 (206) 684-4584,
www.kubotagarden.org, info@kubotagarden.com | Getting there Bus 106 to Renton
Avenue S & 55th Avenue S | Hours Daily dawn–dusk | Tip See more of Fujitaro
Kubota's handiwork at the 150-acre Bloedel Reserve (7571 NE Dolphin Drive,
Bainbridge Island, www.bloedelreserve.org).

60 Kurt Cobain Benches

Unofficial memorial to grunge music icon

On city maps, it's called Viretta Park. The 1.8-acre, grassy slope in the upscale Denny-Blaine neighborhood offers a view out towards Lake Washington. It is named for Viretta Chambers Denny, the daughter-in-law of Seattle pioneer Arthur Denny. To rock fans, though, it is Kurt Cobain Park – or it should be.

In 1994, Cobain, the lead singer and guitarist for the rock band Nirvana, moved into the Queen Anne-style house on the north side of the park with his wife Courtney Love, of the rock band Hole. Not long after, on April 8, 1994, Cobain's body was discovered in the home's greenhouse. Police believe the 27-year-old rock star had shot himself there three days earlier.

Grieving fans and news crews flocked to Viretta Park for a vigil as news of Cobain's death spread. The greenhouse was soon demolished, and in 1997, Love sold the house and moved away. But the musician's admirers continue to make pilgrimages to Viretta Park, especially on the anniversary of his death. They light candles and leave mementos, messages, flowers, small gifts, and graffiti on the two park benches, particularly the one closest to the house, where Cobain may have sat writing song lyrics or just spending time alone with his thoughts.

Over the years, fans have tried getting the park's name changed to honor Cobain or getting a formal memorial to him placed here. But park neighbors are against that idea, and the benches continue to serve as an unofficial memorial.

Before you start eyeing the wooden slats on those benches as potential souvenirs, know that these are not the original Cobain-era benches. The wooden slats from those benches, with all the stickers and heartfelt carvings left by fans, were removed in 2008, installed on new bench frames, and sold at auction in 2014 for $1,500. New wooden slats, now also carved into and graffitied, were attached to the original bench frames.

Address 151 Lake Washington Boulevard E, Seattle, WA 98112, www.seattle.gov/parks/find/parks/viretta-park | Getting there Bus 2 to Madrona Drive & 38th Avenue | Hours Daily 4:30am–11:30pm | Tip Nearby Denny Blaine Park (200 Lake Washington Boulevard E) and Howell Park (1740 Howell Place) both have shoreline views too and are popular with nude bathers.

61 Lake View Cemetery

Bruce and Brandon Lee's final resting place

Incorporated as Seattle Masonic Cemetery in 1872, and redubbed Lake View in 1890, this 42-acre cemetery sits on top of Capitol Hill and offers the deceased and the living glorious views of lakes and mountain ranges.

Most days, you'll find Bruce Lee's fans clustering around his red marble headstone with an inset photo of the martial arts pioneer and pop icon. Lee studied philosophy at the University of Washington. He opened up two martial arts studios in Seattle, and he met his wife Linda here as well. He was buried in this cemetery in 1973, age 32. His son, actor Brandon Lee, who died accidentally while filming a movie in 1993, is buried beside him. Admirers often leave flowers, food items, and tokens on the graves. Cemetery manager Craig Lohr says any coins left on the graves are collected and, with input from the family's estate, used for improvement projects, such as the accessible concrete ramps now at the Lee gravesite.

Look for the graves and family plots of many of the city's earliest settlers on the west side of the cemetery, including Arthur Denny, David Swinson "Doc" Maynard, Henry Yesler, and others whose names you'll spot on streets and parks in town. Nordstrom Department Store co-founder John W. Nordstrom is buried at Lake View, as is Madame Lou Graham, who operated what was said to be an elegant and prosperous bordello in Seattle's Pioneer Square in the late 1800s. Kikisoblu, known as Princess Angeline, rests here too, the eldest daughter of Seattle's namesake, Chief Seattle (Sealth), and is buried beneath a headstone purchased with funds raised by schoolchildren.

There are 46,000 graves here and some wonderful statuary, so pick up a free map with the graves of famous people highlighted. "The cemetery is a wonderful place to visit," says Lohr, "but out of respect for all, we ask that you please stay on pathways."

Address 1554 15th Avenue E, Seattle, WA 98112, +1 (206) 322-1582, www.lakeviewcemeteryassociation.com, information@lakeviewcemetery.com | Getting there Bus 10 to 15th Avenue E & E Galer Street | Hours Call for seasonal visiting hours | Tip Nearby Louisa Boren Park, named for one of Seattle's founding pioneers, also offers great views of Lake Washington and the Cascades (1606 15th Avenue E, www.seattle.gov/parks/find/parks/boren-park).

62 — Last Resort Fire Department

Where to get fired up in Pioneer Square

On June 6, 1889, the story goes, a glue pot boiled over in a downtown Seattle woodworking shop, starting a fire that consumed 25 city blocks of what is now Pioneer Square. Beyond the new fireproof brick buildings and the purchase of the West Coast's first fireboat, reconstruction after the Great Seattle Fire included a better water system and a professional fire department.

Documenting fire department history and maintaining the Pacific Northwest's largest assemblage of firefighting memorabilia and roadworthy firefighting apparatus is the Last Resort Fire Department (LRFD), so named, says retired firefighter and collection co-founder Galen Thomaier because "if all else fails, you can call us."

The LRFD keeps about a dozen early fire trucks in a Ballard garage that's open by appointment. They also host a free firefighting museum in downtown Seattle in the 1928 building that was home to Fire Station #10 and Seattle Fire Department Headquarters for 80 years. The former station watch room now houses historic firefighting photographs and memorabilia, such as early fire extinguishers, uniforms, and nozzles. You'll see eight vintage fire trucks here too, including an 1834 Hunneman hand-drawn pumper, *The Sacramento*, that predates the Great Seattle Fire, and a 1937 Seagrave ladder truck that raced to fires from this exact spot from 1937 to 1961. "Each truck has its own story," says Thomaier, "From the major fires they helped us fight to the firefighters who babied them, worked on them, and whose lives depended on them."

Three chiefs' cars are parked next to the vintage rigs. "They're still active and respond out of here," says Thomaier, "So sometimes the bell rings, the chiefs come down, they turn on the sirens, and head to a fire."

Address 301 2nd Avenue S, Seattle, WA 98104, +1 (206) 783-4474, www.lastresortfd.org, lastresortfd@hotmail.com | Getting there Bus 1, 2, 4, 7 to 3rd Avenue S & S Main Street; Light Rail to Pioneer Square (1 Line) | Hours Thu 11am – 3pm | Tip The Fallen Firefighters Memorial in the adjacent Occidental Park honors four firefighters who died fighting a warehouse fire nearby in 1995 and all other firefighters who have died in the line of duty (117 S Washington Street, www.seattle.gov/fire/about-us/fallen-firefighter-memorial).

63 Lawless Forge

Hammer out a souvenir or a relationship

As a kid, Max Levi wondered how knives were made. His mom didn't know, so she found a blacksmith in their central Pennsylvania town who shared the answer with young Max. Now, as an adult in Seattle, Levi is letting others in on the secret.

At the old-world Lawless Forge studio in the industrial SoDo neighborhood, Levi offers blacksmithing classes that encourage everyone – even kids – to grab tools and transform hot steel into take-home treasures. Affordable introductory public classes last three hours and offer novice forgers the option to make a knife out of a horseshoe, a bottle opener out of a two-foot-long rod, or a coat or towel hook instead of the bottle opener. You can bring your knife home or have it shipped if you're in from farther afield.

Sessions are "fast-paced, but not rushed," says Levi, and they draw couples, friends, families, and out-of-town visitors. "The classes are small and designed to not chew through a person's day. So, within 15 minutes of a class starting, students are swinging hammers and using anvils, tongs, and forges, which are the devices we use to heat the metal."

It sounds more dangerous than it is, says Levi. "But the shop is designed for beginners, and it's not like everyone is running around each other with hot metal." Classes are also safe for first dates. "If you're just getting to know someone, this is something you can do where you'll both start on the same learning level – zero."

Graduates of the basic classes may move on to the one-day, advanced course and learn more about blacksmithing techniques, such as tapering, hot-cutting, twisting, scrolling, and bending. And there is also the option of booking a private class for two people or more to make knives and bottle openers, but to also forge barbecue forks, chopsticks and – a popular option – wedding, anniversary, or friendship rings out of famed Damascus steel.

Address 3600 E Marginal Way S, Seattle, WA 98134, +1 (206) 552-8341, www.lawlessforge.com, info@lawlessforge.com | Getting there By car, take WA-99 S to East Marginal Way S | Hours See website for class schedule | Tip After a class, Levi suggests heading to The Woods tasting room nearby, home to Two Brews Brewing and Seattle Cider, with food by Bread and Circuses (4660 Ohio Avenue S, www.twobeersbrewery.com).

64 Maury Island UFO Mural

Artwork tells the story of an odd encounter

The alleged crash and recovery of an unidentified flying object (UFO) near Roswell, New Mexico in the summer of 1947 is the most well-known UFO incident in US history. But some mysterious sightings in Washington around that time also have a role in "the summer of the saucers."

On June 24, 1947, private pilot Kenneth Arnold sees nine saucer-shaped objects traveling at about 1,200 miles per hour between Mount Rainier and Mount Adams, giving wings to the term "flying saucers." A few days earlier, on June 21, Tacoma resident Harold Dahl, his son, and two crewmen report six flying discs hovering over Dahl's boat in Puget Sound, near Maury Island. Dahl says one low-flying UFO explodes and rains debris on his boat, killing the family dog, damaging the boat, and leaving burns on his son's arm.

Strange happenings continue. Dahl says the next day a "man in black" shows up at his door, warning him to keep mum about the saucers. About a month later, two military intelligence officers crash the B-25 bomber they are flying right after interviewing Dahl and taking samples of the slag rained down by the saucers. Dahl soon claims he made up the whole story. But did he?

Some believe the Maury Island Incident, as it is known, to be true. An award-winning, 2014 film documents this UFO story. And a large mural created to support the film remains on view in Burien, on the side of a shipping container. "I don't believe in the Easter Bunny, Santa Claus, or UFOs," says Nancy Pahl, who was hired to paint the mural with her husband, Zach. "But we put every detail of the story in the mural, down to the dog and the man in black standing on the dock." Whether or not you believe in UFOs, after visiting the mural, walk down the hill to Des Moines Marina Pier. Maury Island is across from the pier, and if there were flying saucers here in 1947, they would have been visible from this spot.

Address 605 S 223rd Street, Des Moines, WA 98198 | **Getting there** By car, take WA-509 S to Des Moines Memorial Drive, SeaTac and continue to S 223rd Street | **Hours** Unrestricted | **Tip** A crashed UFO that may or may not be from the Maury Island incident rests in a field at the Vashon Island Municipal Airport (11130 SW Cove Road, Vashon Island, www.vashon-maury.com/vashon-island/airport).

65__Metsker Maps
Largest retail map shop in the US

In this modern digital age, the global positioning system (GPS) and smartphone apps easily guide you to any destination. But there is still a role for paper maps, atlases, globes, and other cartographic tools that can help chart a path in the world – whether you intend to leave home or not.

That is why geography geeks, world travelers, and day trippers alike visit Metsker Maps, the oldest map store in Seattle and the largest retail map store in the country. In addition to maps for walking in the woods or driving in a city, there are nautical charts for sailing and waterproof maps to take fishing. Historical atlases abound, as do raised relief and antique maps, themed and wood cut maps, globes (including inflatable worlds), and travel books and tools of all kinds.

Who's Metsker? Cartographer Charles Frederick Metsker began making detailed maps of the Pacific Northwest in 1901 and was soon publishing and selling those maps under the moniker 'Metsker the Map Man.' He opened a Metsker Map shop in downtown Seattle in 1950, and in 1999 the company merged with another iconic, geography-minded, local business, the Kroll Map Company, which traces its cartographic roots back to the 1870s.

Today, hiking maps are among the store's best sellers. "Thanks to all the genealogical research people are doing, sales of antique maps are booming too," says Emily Allen, one of the store's long-time employees. She says that while some shoppers need training in how to read a paper map, others pick it up right away. "You can tell a map store is really nostalgic for some people. It reminds them of the good old days, when you'd lay out the map and track your route before setting out on an adventure."

In its current location, Metsker Maps serves another purpose: helping tourists who wander in asking for directions. "We joke about doubling as MapQuest," says Allen.

Address 1511 1st Avenue, Seattle, WA 98101, +1 (206) 623-8747, www.metskers.com, sales@metskers.com | **Getting there** Bus C, D, E, 15, 16 to 3rd Avenue & Pike Street; Light Rail to Westlake (1 Line) | **Hours** Mon–Fri 9am–6pm, Sat & Sun 10am–6pm | **Tip** The 27,000-pound, neon globe adorned with the slogan, "It's in the P-I," still sits on top of the downtown waterfront building that was once the headquarters of the *Seattle Post Intelligencer* newspaper, founded in 1863 and now digital only (101 Elliott Avenue W, www.seattlepi.com).

66 Murder Mementos

Serial killer souvenirs and bits of bygone clowns

If you're sure you're ready, go see a floor-to-ceiling cabinet of curiosities overstuffed with artifacts of all kinds, including a special collection of serial killers' mementos.

Your disturbing voyage of discovery starts on the middle left of the cabinet, where you will see a painting of a skull with a red feather by John Wayne Gacy Jr., the serial killer and sex offender known as the "Killer Clown." While murdering some of his 33 victims, Gacy would sometimes don the "Pogo the Clown" costume he wore to entertain children in hospitals. You'll also spy a small wooden box with keys, cufflinks, and three tins of face paint said to have belonged to him. A typewritten note states, "If you look closely, you can see the killer's fingerprints embedded in the white face paint tin."

Continue on to see an FBI "Wanted" poster for Ted Bundy (see ch. 98), who confessed to killing more than 30 women in Washington and several other states during the 1970s. And don't miss the framed King County Jail commissary order form with which Gary L. Ridgway, known as this region's Green River Killer, once requested a razor, a legal pad, some stamped envelopes, and five pencils.

"It looks to me like he was getting ready to lawyer up," says Todd Hewitt, who curates the collection and owns Big Top Curiosity Shop, where you'll find the cabinet of curiosities and much more.

And then there's "Serial Killer: The Board Game," where players "Pit your demented wits against other serial killers as you test your knowledge in the race to slay five victims and win the game!"

In a nod to Hewitt's affinity for clowns, one cabinet shelf displays a hand in a jar of formaldehyde, labeled as having belonged to one Shady the Clown. "He lost it in a whiskey-driven poker bet with Zardan the Human Pin Cushion," says Hewitt. "And he was never able to perform his world-famous chicken juggling act ever again."

Address 8507 14th Avenue S, Seattle, WA 98108, www.facebook.com/BigTopCuriosity, greatestshoponearth@yahoo.com | Getting there Bus 60 to 14th Avenue S & S Cloverdale Street | Hours Tue–Thu & Sun noon–6pm, Fri & Sat noon–8pm | Tip Refresh your soul and head over to tiny taltalucid Park and Shoreline Habitat, featuring old bridge gears and lovely Duwamish River views (7797 8th Avenue S, www.portseattle.org/places/taltalucid-park-and-shoreline-habitat).

67 __ NW African American Museum

Celebrating African American culture in the PNW

In the early 1980s, word got out that the grand 1909 Colman School building in the Central District was to be closed and razed to make way for a highway. The African American community wanted the building to become a Black history museum instead. And to press the issue, local activists occupied the building in 1985. That occupation stretched to 8 years and became the longest continual occupation of a public building in US history.

Eventually, Seattle's Urban League purchased the building for affordable housing and as a home for the Northwest African American Museum, which opened in 2008. Today, the museum is a vibrant community center and an arts and culture institution celebrating the role of African Americans throughout the Pacific Northwest.

In addition to rotating art and history shows, galleries sing the praises of notable musicians with Pacific Northwest ties, including Quincy Jones, Ernestine Anderson, Esperanza Spalding and, of course, Jimi Hendrix (see ch. 53). The lively jazz and R&B clubs that flourished in the city for many decades are remembered too. Among them is the Old Rocking Chair Club, where in 1948 a teenager named Ray Charles was "discovered" and offered his first recording contract. "Rocking Chair Blues" is Charles' tribute to the venue.

Vintage photos, video kiosks, and artifacts, such as the jacket worn by William H. Holloman, a Tuskegee Airman who went on to become the first African American helicopter pilot in the US Air Force, inform visitors about the experiences and contributions of African Americans in the Pacific Northwest to art, aviation, business, labor history, and much more from the late 1700s to the present. Included is the story of George Washington Bush, one of the earliest permanent settlers in Washington Territory.

REPORTING FOR DUTY

"I wouldn't have missed being a Tuskegee cadet for the world. It was a proud tradition. My love of flying and the opportunity to serve my country prompted me to reach for the stars in my own way."

—AL COLVIN

WORLD WAR II
IN THE NORTHWEST

As the United States entered World War II in 1941, African Americans in the Northwest joined the war effort in many different ways. As the number of war-related jobs exploded, Black workers and their families flocked to the region—to jobs in Seattle's aircraft factories, Portland's shipyards, and Hanford's nuclear reservation. Many others joined the service, swelling the ranks of Northwest military bases, or fighting overseas.

Address 2300 S Massachusetts Street, Seattle, WA 98144, 1 + (206) 518-6000, www.naamnw.org, info@naamnw.org | Getting there Bus 7 to Rainier Avenue S & S State Street. Free museum lot parking. | Hours Wed–Sat 10am–5pm (open until 7pm on the first Thu of each month) | Tip Stroll through Jimi Hendrix Park, adjacent to the museum, to see the purple-hued Shadow Wave Wall featuring a portrait of the musical artist (2400 S Massachusetts Street, www.jimihendrixparkfoundation.org).

68 Off the Rez Café

Modern spin on Native American cuisine

Cecilia Rikard and her life and business partner, Mark McConnell, wanted to join the local food truck scene with something new. They drew on McConnell's Native American heritage, cultural connections from his mom's childhood on Montana's Blackfeet Indian Reservation, and his fondness for the frybread and Indian tacos served at family gatherings and powwows. The couple rolled out their instantly popular, turquoise Off the Rez Food Truck in 2012, with a menu of frybreads served with sweet toppings or as "Indian tacos," filled with chicken chile verde or pulled pork. "Seattle's Native community was excited to see that," says Rikard. "It reminded them of home."

The truck is still rolling, and now there is also a brick and mortar Off the Rez Café in the lobby of the Burke Museum of Natural History and Culture, with a longer menu and views onto landscaping that includes fossils and more than 80,000 native plants.

Seattle's first Native American café is a perfect match for the Burke, which became the state's first official museum in 1899 and moved into a stunning new $106 million building in 2019. The new Burke has real and very rare dinosaur fossils, visible labs and workrooms, and six galleries telling the history of the people, landscape, plants, and animals of the Pacific Northwest. "Part of the Burke's mission is to educate people on the Native aspects of Washington's inception," says Rickard, "So for the café menu, we kept the frybread and the Indian tacos but added dishes that use ingredients that were part of the traditional indigenous diet, such as wild rice and braised bison, and we added our own modern spin."

This is Seattle, so it is a given that espresso drinks and teas are on the menu. But Off the Rez adds its spin here too, with a special take on a traditional cedar tea made with dried and crushed cedar, blackberries, and black tea.

Address The Burke Museum, 4300 15th Avenue NE, Seattle, WA 98105, +1 (206) 414-8226, www.offthereztruck.com, catering@offthereztruck.com | **Getting there** Bus 48 to 15th Avenue NE & NE 45th Street | **Hours** Tue–Sun 10am–5pm | **Tip** ʔálʔal Café in Pioneer Square is a social enterprise bistro serving Indigenous ingredients from various regions of North America (122 2nd Avenue S, www.alalcafe.org).

69 __ Oriental Mart

James Beard Award winner with a side of sass

Don't be intimidated by Oriental Mart's many handwritten signs of admonishment at the lunch counter, such as *Your portion depends on your attitude. I mean it!* Or, *To all u knuckleheads, Don't talk 2 me while I'm cooking.* The family-run mainstay at Pike Place Market is part souvenir shop, part Asian grocery, part homestyle Filipino restaurant, and 100% welcoming.

Diners are advised to put their meal orders in the hands of Leila Rosas, or "Ate Lei," as she is known to regulars. Rosas' mom opened the small grocery in 1971 after the family came to Seattle from the Philippines. In 1987, Rosas set up a kitchen in the back of the store to show shoppers how to make Filipino dishes using ingredients on the shelves. An 18-seat lunch counter grew out of that idea, with a no-menu policy. *We don't have a menu 'cus… I cook what I want. (Depends on my mood),* explains one of the restaurant's many signs about how things are done here.

Regulars rave about Rosas' chicken *adobo* and the *pancit*, a Filipino noodle dish. The "Do You Trust Me" plate is a heaping serving of what Rosas decides to cook for you. She makes her salmon *sinigang* using tamarind broth, mustard greens, and salmon collars brought to her by the crew at the famed fish-tossers at Pike Place Fish Market across the street. And despite a sign that warns, *If u don't know how to eat our salmon sinigang don't order it,* Rosas will teach you how to enjoy the dish that helped the Orient Mart gain a coveted "America's Classics Award" from the James Beard Foundation in 2020. The honor, bestowed on a half-dozen American restaurants each year that have "timeless appeal" and "serve quality food that reflects the character of their communities" was a surprise to Rosas. But she says it doesn't mean she's changing her no-menu policy, taking down the snarky signs, or moving the lunch counter to a fancier spot.

Address 1506 Pike Place, Shop No. 509, Seattle, WA 98101, +1 (206) 622-8488 | Getting there Bus C, D, 15 to 3rd Avenue & Pike Street; Light Rail to Westlake (1 Line) | Hours Daily 11am–3pm | Tip Grab a great cup of coffee at Ghost Alley Espresso across from the icky Gum Wall (1499 Post Alley, www.ghostalleyespresso.com).

70 Pacific Fishermen Shipyard

Bounty of Ballard's history in salvaged signs

Unless you have a connection with the local maritime industry or sail a boat through the Ballard Locks, you might not pay any attention to the Pacific Fishermen Shipyard on the Lake Washington Ship Canal. But this full-service boat yard is both a part of Seattle's history and an informal keeper of the neighborhood's commercial past.

The property, at the corner of the 24th Avenue NW and the canal, opened as a shipyard in 1871. Over the years, its workers have built and serviced everything from sternwheelers, tugboats, ferries, and fishing boats to Navy minesweepers, small cruise ships, mega yachts, and other vessels. Since 1946, the shipyard has been an unusual co-op corporation created by about 400 Norwegian heritage fishermen and their families, who each chipped in $300 to purchase the operation from the Ballard Marine Railway Company.

Like the maritime industry, the neighborhood around the shipyard has been changing. Once populated chiefly by Scandinavian migrants working as farmers, fishers, boat builders, and loggers, Ballard is now home to young professionals, who frequent modern coffee shops, gourmet restaurants, tattoo parlors, and hipster bars. But "Old Ballard" is not forgotten. Dozens of salvaged neon and wooden signs that once advertised iconic and now shuttered stores, restaurants, and lots of bars, such as the Viking Tavern, The People's Pub, Zesto's, and Ballard Bait and Tackle, are displayed in the shipyard's courtyard.

Former shipyard general manager Doug Dixon says some signs were purchased or left at the gate, while others were "adopted" after they "somehow" dropped into the bed of his pickup truck when he was driving past defunct venues in the wee hours. It's probably best not to ask too many questions. The best time to stop by is at dusk or in the evening, when many of the neon signs are aglow.

Address 5351 24th Avenue NW, Seattle, WA 98107, +1 (206) 784-2562, www.pacificfishermen.com, info@pfishipyard.com | Getting there Bus 17, 18, 29, 40, 44 to NW Market Street & Ballard Avenue NW | Hours Unrestricted from the street | Tip Learn more about Ballard's Scandinavian history and grab a Nordic treat at the National Nordic Museum around the corner (2655 NW Market Street, www.nordicmuseum.org).

71 Panama Hotel & Tea House

Unclaimed baggage tells a tragic story

The Panama Hotel Tea & Coffee House serves coffee, Japanese pastries, and more than 40 different types of teas. It also preserves history.

Before World War II, when the US government forcibly sent people of Japanese origins from West Coast cities to internment camps inland, the Panama Hotel sat at the hub of Seattle's Nihonmachi (Japan Town) neighborhood, in what is now the Chinatown-International District. Designed by Sabro Ozasa, Seattle's first Japanese American architect, and completed in 1910, the building originally hosted a tailor, a dentist, and other businesses on the ground floor and three floors of single occupancy guest rooms above, providing housing for fishermen, laborers, and Japanese immigrants. In the basement were two *sentos*, traditional Japanese public bathhouses – one for men and one for women, each with multiple soaking tubs. Today, the hotel is a budget Airbnb lodging and offers tours of the intact but not operating Hashidate-Yu below ground, said to be the only surviving *sento* in the country.

As many Japanese community members were being rushed to the camps during the war, Panama Hotel owner Takashi Hori allowed neighbors to store possessions in the hotel's basement. It was assumed that families would return to retrieve their belongings when the war was over. Many did not. Hori, who was also sent to a camp, kept his neighbor's belongings in storage for years, just in case.

In 1985, Jan Johnson bought the hotel from Hori and his family and tried to reunite storeroom items with their owners or their descendants. What remains is now an informal museum of the community as it was before World War II. In the tea house, historic photographs, maps, signs, framed letters, and ephemera line the walls, and visitors may view some of the still unclaimed belongings through a plexiglass window that has been cut into the original wood floor.

Address 605 S Main Street, Seattle, WA 98104, +1 (206) 223-9242, www.panamahotelseattle.com, reservations@panamahotelseattle.com | Getting there Light Rail to International District/ Chinatown (1 Line); bus 7, 14 to S Jackson Street & Maynard Avenue S | Hours Daily 9am–4pm | Tip The Asian supermarket Uwajimaya's flagship store is nearby, with a wonderful gift section, restaurants, and a branch of Japan's Kinokuniya Bookstore (600 5th Avenue S, www.uwajimaya.com/stores/seattle).

72 __ Paramount Theater Library

Archive of Seattle's entertainment history

Seattle is dotted with historic theaters dating back to the early 1900s, many of which have been returned to their original grandeur. Three gems on the list – The Paramount, The Moore, and the Neptune Theatre – are owned and/or operated by the non-profit Seattle Theatre Group (STG), which takes seriously the storied role these venues had and continue to play in the city's arts and culture scene.

The Paramount, the most ornate of the trio, opened in 1928 as an opulent movie palace. Still in place is the grand Wurlitzer organ that played during silent movie programs. The theater escaped the wrecking ball in the late 1980s and is restored to its former glory with modern improvements that include mechanics for a unique system that can tuck all the main floor seating away for flat flooring during events. You can learn about The Paramount's rebirth during free monthly tours, or you can visit the STG Archive and Gallery next door, which documents every performance at all three theaters and houses memorabilia, playbills, and autographed pictures and posters.

Included in the collection is a treasure trove of items discovered during the renovation of The Moore, which opened in 1907 and is Seattle's oldest operating theater. For many years The Moore had a segregated balcony for Black audiences accessed by a separate side entrance. "It was the same show, but a different experience," says Mason Sherry, STG's senior theater manager. "They had their own concessions, their own ushers, and their own bathrooms." The original balcony seating was heavy, wooden pews with spaces that were later covered with leather. "When we removed the coverings to replace the seating we found a time capsule inside the benches," says Sherry. "Everything from tickets and hat pins, to photos, dice, some coins, and many pristine programs dating from 1907 to 1934."

Address Paramount Theater Building, 911 Pine Street, Seattle, WA 98101,
+1 (206) 812-3304, www.stgpresents.org/library, library@stgpresents.org | Getting there
Bus 11, 49 to Pine Street & 9th Avenue; Light Rail Westlake Center (1 Line) | Hours
Library Tue 10am–2pm; Theater tours 1st Sat of the month at 10am | Tip Town Hall
Seattle hosts many arts, science, and civic events for free or $5 from its grand, historic,
former church building (1119 8th Avenue, www.townhallseattle.org).

73 Patent Tree

Lots of winning ideas

Seattle and the Central Puget Sound region have long been hotbeds of innovation. United Parcel Service (UPS) was born here in 1907. Later came Boeing, Costco, Amazon, Starbucks, and Microsoft. The creativity that drives innovation also spurs invention. In fact, as Seattle's Museum of History and Industry (MOHAI) points out, since 1860, the U.S. Patent Office has granted more than 15,000 patents to inventors in the region, "a statistic that makes us one of the most inventive places in the United States."

While some inventions that hail from here never quite caught on, others certainly have. In 1922, Bremerton's Lloyd "Trapper" Nelson made hiking a more pleasant prospect by designing, building, and marketing a wood-framed, canvas backpack. In 1936, Eddie Bauer invented the goose down-filled parka after almost freezing to death in a wet wool garment. And a fully automated car wash system was invented by Seattle brothers Archie, Dean, and Eldon Anderson in 1951. Pickleball, a game blending tennis, badminton, and ping-pong, was cooked up by Joel Pritchard, Bill Bell, and Barney McCallum of Bainbridge Island in 1965. And in 2008, Mark Oblack and Mariel Head invented the ChuckIt, a plastic wand that allows pet owners to throw tennis balls for dogs over and over, without dealing with pet slobber.

You will spot some of these inventions, along with patents for an umbrella (1914), a metal lamp post (1932), and a restaurant with a rotating floor (1964), on MOHAI's Patent Tree, a 3-D exhibit with illustrations and information about 70 local patents. While in MOHAI's Grand Atrium, be sure to look up to see another Seattle-made invention: the 1919 B-1 seaplane that made international airmail runs between Seattle and Vancouver, BC for eight years, outlasting six engines. This was the Boeing Company's first commercial airplane and the only one of its kind ever built.

Address Lake Union Park, 860 Terry Avenue N, Seattle, WA 98109, +1 (206) 324-1126, www.mohai.org | Getting there Bus C, 40, 64 to Westlake Avenue N & Mercer Street; South Lake Union Streetcar to Lake Union Park | Hours Daily 10am–5pm | Tip Contemplate your next invention at seafood-forward Westward on the north shore of Lake Union (2501 N Northlake Way, www.westwardseattle.com).

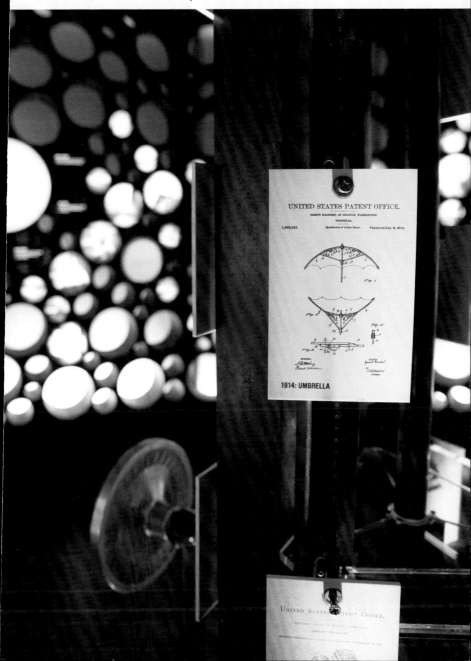

74 Pilling's Pond

Everything at this pond is just ducky

It looks like an urban pond with dozens of happy ducks – and it is. But Pilling's Pond in Licton Springs is also a nationally known urban waterfowl reserve, a half-acre wildlife sanctuary, and a fiercely protected community treasure with a charming backstory.

In the mid-1920s, when Chuck Pilling was about 12 years old, he needed a home for three ducks. So he dug a hole on his family's dairy farm north of the city and tapped into water from nearby Licton Springs. When he was older and living on the property with his wife, he expanded the pond to accommodate his growing interest and self-taught expertise in breeding wild ducks in captivity.

As the area around it developed, Pilling's pond remained an oasis of trees, wild grasses, handmade nesting boxes, and other waterfowl-friendly amenities. Pilling spent seven decades here, studying, feeding, caring for, and breeding ducks. He was the first to breed several species in captivity, including hooded mergansers, buffleheads, and harlequin ducks. He supplied sought-after ducklings to major zoos around the world, including the Smithsonian National Zoological Park in Washington, DC.

After Pilling died in 2001, a childhood friend and neighbor, David Kunkle, cared for the property until his death in 2018. The current owners rent to dedicated, onsite caretakers who make sure the wild, semi-wild, and resident ducks at Pilling's Pond are well-fed, healthy, and able to successfully raise their ducklings every spring and summer. "The goal is to make it a great place for any species of duck to splash down for an hour or a year," says former caretaker Michael McKeirnan, "It doesn't exactly look like Disneyland, but we do what we can to keep the birds happy."

Visitors can learn the history of the site from a large wooden sign and look through the fence to see Pilling's ducks paddling, splashing, and enjoying his pond.

Address N 90th Street between Densmore & Ashworth Avenues N, Seattle, WA 98101, www.pillings-pond.org, info@pillings-pond.org | Getting there Bus 20 to Wallingford Avenue N & N 90th Street | Hours Dawn–dusk from the outside only | Tip The creek feeding Pilling's Pond runs through nearby Licton Springs Park, once a healing center for Native Americans (9536 Ashworth Avenue N, www.seattle.gov/parks/find/parks/licton-springs-park).

75 __The Pinball Museum

Play through the decades

In 2008, Cindy and Charlie Martin needed an after-dinner activity more interesting than watching TV. A pinball machine in the garage was the answer. "We played it for a while, and it broke," says Charlie, "I told Cindy I was going to get another one, and pretty soon the garage was full of pinball machines." The couple considered a pinball club with friends but decided instead to squeeze more than 50 vintage pinball machines from their growing collection into a narrow International District storefront they dubbed the Seattle Pinball Museum.

The admission fee allows you to stay and play for hours. And you'll learn a few things along the way. Charlie Martin says there are differences between an arcade and this carefully organized pinball museum. "An arcade doesn't have information cards posted by each machine to tell you the year it was made, the manufacturer, the artist, how many were produced, or the differences between machines. And an arcade doesn't have the machines in chronological order from the 1960s on to give a view of American culture and society over the years."

An early machine from the 1960s called "The Texan" sports a handsome cowboy on the back glass and wooden railings with metal holders for players' cigarettes. Popular machines from the 1970s celebrate Elton John's "Captain Fantastic" and The Who's "Pinball Wizard." Outer space is the theme reflected in some machines from the 1980s that have "black holes" and playing fields that look like the moon. And machines from the 1990s portray popular bands and TV shows, including Guns N' Roses and The Simpsons.

To get the most of your visit, the Martins suggest starting with the early machines and playing by decade to see how styles and technology change. To improve your score, they say nudging the machines is fine (the tilts are set to medium). And when in doubt, "Just shoot for the flashing lights."

Address 508 Maynard Avenue S, Seattle, WA 98104, +1 (206) 623-0759, www.seattlepinballmuseum.com, info@seattlepinballmuseum.com | Getting there Bus 7, 14, 36 to S Jackson Street & Maynard Avenue S; Light Rail to International District/Chinatown (1 Line); First Hill Streetcar to 7th & Jackson/Chinatown | Hours Fri–Mon noon–6pm | Tip There's a quirky arcade inside Shorty's, an unconventional, circus-themed bar in Belltown (2316 2nd Avenue, www.shortydog.com).

76 Rage Industry
You're encouraged to bust stuff up

No matter how mellow you are, there are sure to be times when anger, fury, or the day's frustrations build up and make you feel like hauling off and breaking something. But you likely hold back for fear of ruining something valuable – or landing in jail. The folks at Rage Industry get it. And that is why they offer a space where you can safely and legally throw stuff against a brick wall or use a variety of tools to smash things. They will even clean up the mess.

What can you break? For each session, participants get to pick out a variety of small, medium, and large items from a well-stocked pantry that offers bottles, glassware, household decorations, ceramics, and other objects that will be fun to break. For an extra fee, guests can add TVs, printers and other electronics, furniture, or toilets (the most popular). You can also BYOB – bring your own box of items calling out to be broken too, like those carefully framed photos of you and your ex – as long as the box fits through the door.

"In addition to stressed out and frustrated people, we get a lot of couples who are on their first dates, as well as people going through divorces," explains Rage Industry manager Brian Op. Birthday and bachelorette parties are also quite popular.

It may feel odd at first, but once you get started, you will find that breaking stuff is surprisingly satisfying and can provide a safe, physical release that is heartily approved of by some therapists. But it can also be dangerous, with flying shards and other people breaking stuff around you. So Rage Industry requires that guests wear long pants and closed shoes. "There WILL be glass on the floor," is a listed advisory.

They will supply all the protective gear you and your friends will need, including coveralls, gloves, face shields, and vests. They also provide a selection of hammers, golf clubs, pans, sledgehammers, crowbars, and other useful implements of destruction.

Address 13333 Lake City Way NE, Seattle, WA 98125, +1 (206) 678-2133,
www.rageindustry.com, seattlerageindustry@gmail.com | Getting there Bus 320, 322, 330
to Lake City Way NE & NE 130th Street | Hours By appointment only | Tip You can
also work off some rage with axe throwing at Seattle's branch of Blade & Timber
(206 E Broadway, www.bladeandtimber.com).

77 REI Flagship Store

Prep for adventure and spot a time capsule

Today, there are countless outdoor equipment stores. But when REI (Recreational Equipment, Incorporated) started back in 1938, it blazed a trail by offering Seattle-based adventurers access to good deals on high-quality gear. REI's first retail outlet was a shelf in a local co-op store. Today, the company's Seattle flagship store covers an entire city block. It's both an outfitting mecca and a destination for urban adventures. You don't have to shop to enjoy your visit there.

Outside the store is a lush urban forest, with 54 types of native trees and flora, as well as a pond, a 33-foot-tall waterfall that masks the sound of the nearby highway, and a test track for mountain bikes – REI's latest models or your own. Inside is a three-story treehouse for kids, a giant compass built into the second story floor, and an in-store National Park Service Ranger Station, where you can purchase recreation passes and maps, and even secure a permit to cut down a Christmas tree on park lands.

For most visitors, the iconic feature of the store is the 65-foot-tall climbing pinnacle, which is built with 4.5 miles of rebar. Solo, group, and class climbs are offered. Those who make it to the top are rewarded with views of the Seattle skyline and, on clear days, glimpses of the surrounding mountain ranges. There is also a treat for those who look down. What even few REI store employees know is that there is a time capsule in the floor beneath a plaque at the southwest corner of the pinnacle enclosure. Placed there during the store's grand opening in 1996, the capsule includes grand opening materials signed by people who were there, sales flyers, a copy of a book published on REI's 50th anniversary in 1988, and a floppy disk that will likely stump those who gather around for the opening of the time capsule on September 13, 2046, the 50th anniversary of the store's opening.

Address 222 Yale Avenue N, Seattle, WA 98109, +1 (206) 223-1944, www.rei.com/stores/
seattle | Getting there Bus 216, 218, 257, 268 to Stewart Street & Yale Avenue N | Hours
Mon–Sat 9am–9pm, Sun 10am–7pm | Tip Find public art, interpretive exhibits, a dog
park, and more urban adventures at the block-long Seattle City Light Denny Substation
two blocks away (1250 Denny Way, www.seattle.gov/light/dennysub).

78_ Retired Air Raid Tower

A Cold War relic in the heart of Phinney Park

In the early 1950s, with the Cold War and fears of nuclear attacks in the news, many cities around the country revived and upgraded neighborhood air raid systems in the hopes of being able to give citizens advance warning of impending danger.

Seattle officials did their part by taking small World War II-era sirens out of storage and installing them and 21 powerful new sirens around town, including many that were mounted on tall steel towers. Most of those sirens and towers have since been scrapped. But you can spot one today atop a 45-foot-tall tower at the center of tiny Heart of Phinney Park, next to the Phinney Center.

When this tower was installed in 1953, the center's buildings housed the John B. Allen elementary school. Each Wednesday at noon, when the five-horsepower, gas-powered, nearly six-ton siren dubbed "Big Bertha" was tested, students at the school were instructed to curl up under their desks as part of the "duck and cover" drills they had learned. Those weekly, noontime tests continued until the early 1970s and consisted of more than five minutes of loud tones and long, blaring sound blasts. The sirens could be heard more than a mile away, including at the nearby Woodland Park Zoo, a site that was considered but rejected as the initial, much louder, installation site for fear of alarming the animals.

Thankfully silent now, this decommissioned air raid tower, with its bright-yellow siren, now serves as a symbol of peace, especially during the winter holidays, when it is draped with thousands of LED lights to serve as the neighborhood's non-denominational "Glo-Cone." The park also provides stone benches with quotes carved into them and several chess tables. Loaner chess pieces are available in adjacent Phinney Center, which is also home to an art gallery, a tool lending library, a community woodshop, and legend has it, some resident ghosts.

Address 6532 Phinney Avenue N, Seattle, WA 98103, +1 (206) 783-2244, www.phinneycenter.org, pna@phinneycenter.org | Getting there Bus 5 to Phinney Avenue N & N 67th Street | Hours Unrestricted | Tip You can visit another remnant air raid tower by the parking lot at Northacres Park in the Haller Lake neighborhood (12718 1st Avenue NE, www.seattle.gov/parks/find/parks/northacres-park).

79_Rubber Chicken Museum

All the wacky stuff at Archie McPhee

Do you need squirrel underpants, a box of eyeball finger puppets, or a unicorn lunchbox? Probably not. But you will want them all, and maybe a bacon-scented air freshener and a wind-up pigeon too, after visiting the kooky and kitschy Archie McPhee store in Seattle's Wallingford neighborhood. Shelves, bins, and barrels overflow with carefully organized inventory that includes odd-flavored candies, quirky costumes, inflatable furniture, wacky games, gags, and thousands of other odd and intriguing items that are all for sale. But in this entertaining emporium, the action goes beyond shopping.

Everyone gets a free present on their birthday. There are fortune-telling machines and a chamber where everything glows in the dark. A strange Feejee Mermaid-like creature the staff captured in 2010 and named the Wallingford Beast is on display behind plexiglass. And a cabinet dubbed, "Room 6," is filled with vintage novelty items from the collection of Archie McPhee founder Mark Pahlow.

The free-entry Rubber Chicken Museum at the rear of the store displays more than 200 bright yellow examples of comedy's favorite squawking poultry prop. It is hard to miss the seven-foot-tall rubber chicken, but you will have to look closely to see the world's smallest (about a centimeter) and second smallest (about one inch). Other highlights of the collection include a flattened rubber chicken found in the company warehouse, a glow-in-the-dark rubber chicken, old-style silent rubber chickens, and many modern ones that squeak, squawk, and squall.

"Rubber chickens are certainly hilarious," says Shana Danger, whose official corporate title was High Priestess of Rubber Chickens even before she became the Rubber Chicken Museum curator. "But they're also serious. They have a long history in pop culture and are connected to many personal stories from work and home."

Address 1300 N 45th Street, Seattle, WA 98103, +1 (206) 297-0240, www.archiemcpheeseattle.com, mcphee@mcphee.com | **Getting there** Bus 44, 62 to N 45th Street & Stone Way N | **Hours** Daily 11am–6pm | **Tip** The original scoop shop for Molly Moon's Homemade Ice Cream, which sources local ingredients and donates to food banks and local non-profits, is up the street (1622.5 N 45th Street, www.mollymoon.com).

80_ Scarecrow Video

Be kind and rewind in the 21st century

During the 1980s and 90s, home entertainment might involve a trip to a neighborhood video rental store or a branch of Blockbuster or Hollywood Video. Spending an hour or more browsing the titles and getting staff tips before settling on a movie – or three – to take home and return a few days later was part of the ritual. The internet and streaming services, such as Netflix, Hulu, and Amazon Prime, each of which might offer a few thousand titles at a time, put an end to video rental stores.

However, in Seattle, you can still walk into Scarecrow video and rent from an inventory of more 140,000 films and television programs on VHS, DVS, Blue-ray, and other formats, including many titles available nowhere else. Founded in 1988 by the late George Latsios, who began renting his video collection to friends and then to others from the back of a record store, Scarecrow has morphed into a non-profit organization, offering the largest collection of publicly available videos in the world. Hundreds of new titles are added each week, and nothing is ever deleted from the collection. Scarecrow also sells movie merch and candy, rents via mail, and hosts free programs in the screening room. "It's film nerd heaven," says Scarecrow operations manager Jamie Han.

There are themed sections – sometimes entire rooms – for everything from adventure, comedy, romance, and drama to murder, mystery, war, westerns and more. Not sure where to start or if the film you are after is as good as it seems? You can look through the digital inventory or browse the books and binders in "Knowledge Central," the in-house library. Better yet, ask the movie maniacs on the staff. They can help you find what you want, or what you did not know you needed to see. "If you ask for *Sleepless in Seattle*, we might also suggest some other Nora Ephron movies, but no one will get made fun of here," says Han. "It's not like the movie *Clerks*. There is no snark."

Address 5030 Roosevelt Way NE, Seattle, WA 98105, +1 (206) 524-8554, www.scarecrow.com, scarecrow@scarecrow.com | Getting there Bus 67 to Roosevelt Way NE & NE 50th Street | Hours Tue, Thu–Sun noon–8pm, Wed noon–10pm | Tip Scenes from *Singles* and *10 Things I Hate About You* were filmed in Gas Works Park, at the south end of the Fremont neighborhood (2101 N Northlake Way, www.seattle.gov/parks/find/parks/gas-works-park).

81 Schmitz Preserve Park
Old growth in the city

Before white settlers arrived in this region and began cutting down all the trees, there were vast forests filled with towering old-growth trees, many of them hundreds of years old. Two Seattle parks still offer a glimpse of what those forests may have looked like. Best known is the 'Magnificent Forest' in Seward Park, southeast of downtown, which is home to the largest stand of old growth trees in the city.

Smaller and less well-known is the 53-acre Schmitz Preserve Park in West Seattle, not far from Alki Beach. Between 1908 and 1912, with forest lands around Seattle disappearing quickly, civic leader and park commissioner Ferdinand Schmitz and his wife, Emma, donated 30-acres of undeveloped ravine for a park they wanted preserved in its natural state. The city later added some more acres, and, although a few trees have been logged, Schmitz Preserve Park is an urban old-growth forest today.

1.7 miles of trails and wooden foot bridges meander and loop through the park past massive Douglas firs, western hemlocks, and western red cedars. Trails are often muddy, so wear proper boots. Downed trees, which would have been cut up and removed in more manicured parks, lie where they fell, and many giant stumps and rotting timbers now serve as nurse logs, offering nourishment and encouragement for a new generation of trees. Along the paths, you'll see and hear the work of red-tufted pileated woodpeckers, whacking big holes in dead trees as they search for bugs. And, depending on the season, you'll see salmonberries, skunk cabbage, wild ginger, and other flora on the forest floor.

By Schmitz Park Bridge, spanning the park's ravine, a 79-step, wooden stairway leads down to the creek bed. Look for the gallery of graffiti at the base of the bridge and the remains of a crocodile painted on some fallen logs by the north entrance to the preserve.

Address 5551 SW Admiral Way, Seattle, WA 98116, www.seattle.gov/parks/find/parks/schmitz-preserve-park | Getting there Bus 50, 56 to SW Admiral Way & 57th Avenue SW | Hours Daily 6am–10pm | Tip Alki Playground on the edge of the park features the popular whale tail sculpture and a play area accessible for kids of all abilities (5817 SW Lander Street, www.seattle.gov/parks/find/parks/alki-playground).

82 __ Seattle Asian Art Museum

Heads of divine bodies and a weeping Buddha

Seattle's Asian Art Museum (SAAM), an arm of the Seattle Art Museum (SAM), fills the 1933 Art Deco landmark building in Volunteer Park that once housed all of SAM's holdings.

During a major renovation, SAAM did away with grouping artwork by country or by period and now organizes exhibitions by broad themes, such as color and play, clothing, nature, worship, birth, and death. In the "Divine Bodies" gallery, for example, a thousand-armed, 11-headed, 16th-century Guanyin statue from China shares space with 11 vitrines filled with heads made from bronze, lacquer, limestone, and other materials.

"Many museums place sculpted Buddha heads in a row. We tweaked this convention slightly in showing a variety of figures originally for both Buddhist and Hindu worship, from multiple geographic origins, and from different time periods," explains Foong Ping, SAAM's Foster Foundation Curator of Chinese Art. "Side-by-side, a viewer becomes sensitive to the complex reality of how notions of ideal, divine beauty vary. If the pieces convey serenity or elegance, each does so in such different ways."

This gallery also houses the seated Buddha Shakyamuni, cast in the late 8th to early 9th century in Kashmir. The sculpture stayed in storage for many years because it had a condition that caused it to be covered in moisture, prompting SAAM staff to refer to it as their "Weeping Buddha." Fortunately, this Buddha is now viewable in a special glass case filled with gas that allows it to be displayed tear-free.

The camels flanking SAAM's doors are replicas of the iconic originals, which are now at SAM downtown. For a kick, watch the 1985 neo-noir film *Trouble in Mind*, starring Kris Kristofferson, Keith Carradine, Geneviève Bujold, Lori Singer, and a not-in-drag Divine. An epic party/shoot-out scene was filmed inside the museum's building.

Address 1400 East Prospect Street, Seattle, WA 98112, +1 (206) 654-3210, www.seattleartmuseum.org | Getting there Bus 10 to 15th Avenue E & E Highland Drive | Hours Fri–Sun 10am–5pm | Tip Isamu Noguchi's 1969 *Black Sun* sculpture sits across from SAAM's entry and is sited so that its open center provides picture-perfect views of the Space Needle, the Olympic Mountains, and Elliott Bay (www.noguchi.org/artworks/public-works).

83 Seattle Chocolate Factory

Where tasting chocolate is an experience

If you like sweets, Seattle's chocolate scene has you covered. Gourmet shops include Theo Chocolate's flagship store and factory tour in Fremont; Indi Chocolate's café and factory in Pike Place Market; and Fran's shop and factory in University Village and Georgetown – to name just a few.

And then there's Seattle Chocolate Company, with its factory and store near Southcenter. This woman-owned and run company uses ethically sourced cacao and has two brands: Seattle Chocolate and jcoco. The Seattle Chocolate line has more than 20 types of two-bite truffles, plus truffle bars with creative flavor combinations and Pacific Northwest names, such as Rainy Day Espresso, Overcast Sea Salt, and Rainier Cherry. The jcoco premium line features epicurean-inspired chocolate bars, such as crisp quinoa sesame and mango plantain, and 10 percent of net profits are donated to food bank partners locally and nationally.

"Eating chocolate is an incredibly sensory experience," says Jean Thompson, Seattle Chocolate CEO and owner, and the "J" in jcoco. In her step-by-step guide to enjoying great chocolate, she suggests holding your nose and putting a square or small bite in your mouth. "See what you can taste and feel at this stage," she says. "After the chocolate melts a bit on your tongue, unplug your nose and let the complex flavors rush in. Smell is crucial to tasting chocolate, and your nose allows you to taste the different flavor dimensions."

You can find the chocolates in a branded store at SEA airport and around town. The flagship store has a colorful bulk truffle bar, all chocolates in production, wine for pairings, and in-store exclusives. Stop by on Saturdays for bags of imperfect chocolates at a significant discount. Factory tours take place on a hot pink walkway above the factory floor, with lots of chocolate tasting. Tours are haunted in October.

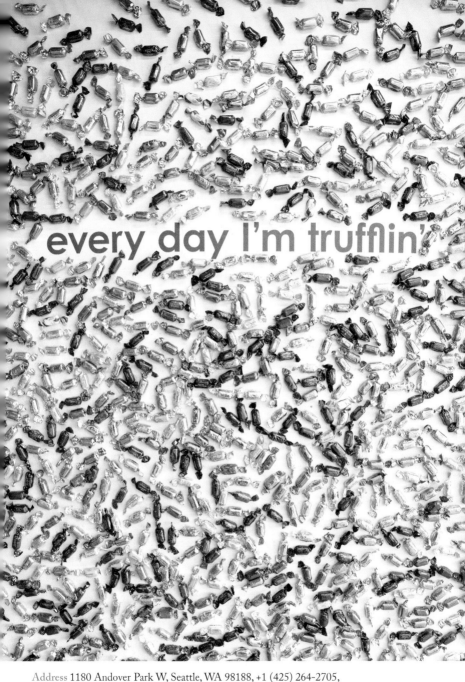

every day I'm trufflin'

Address 1180 Andover Park W, Seattle, WA 98188, +1 (425) 264-2705, www.seattlechocolate.com | Getting there Bus 150 to Andover Park W & S 180th Street | Hours Mon–Fri 10am–6pm, Sat 10am–5pm | Tip Intrigue Chocolate in Pioneer Square handcrafts small batches of craft chocolate (157 S Jackson Street, www.intriguechocolate.com).

84 Seattle Meowtropolitan

Sip a catpuccino and adopt your new best friend

Cat cafés, where customers come to have a coffee or cocktails and then stay to play with cats, got their start in 1998, when the world's first such cat canoodling venue opened in Taiwan. Soon after, the trend became the cat's meow and spread to Japan, Europe, Canada, and the United States.

Seattle joined the kitty club in December 2015 with Seattle Meowtropolitan. The café side of this feline-centric spot serves cat-themed food and drinks, including catpuccinos and meowchas. The adjacent cat lounge is home to resident cats and adoptable ones from Regional Animal Services of King County (RASKC). For first-timers, Seattle Meowtropolitan partner Andrew Hsieh notes that the café "isn't like a dog park." He says some people arrive with their own cats in tow, hoping to have their kitties mingle with the cats on-site. "But if you know anything about cats, it's very rare that you can throw a new cat into a group of other cats and have them be OK. They need time to come to an understanding," says Hsieh.

Instead, he says you can come here, have some coffee and treats, and then book a session, for a nominal price, to hang out with the cats in the lounge for half an hour or so. The resident cats, known as the Knights of Meowtropolitan (a nod to *Game of Thrones*) are friendly felines and well-suited to café life's constant stream of visitors. The adoptable cats are usually six months old or older and are helpfully described by color and personality to help facilitate good matches. Rambunctious Red cats are "spirited, independent thinkers," while Bashful Blue cats are apt to be nervous in new situations and cautious about coming out of their shells. The Easy-Going Green cats? They are already carefree kitties ready to go with the flow.

Seattle Meowtropolitan also hosts special events, such as yoga with cats and, come Halloween, pumpkin carving under the super-vision of cats.

Address 1225 N 45th Street, Seattle, WA 98103, +1 (206) 632-2330, www.seameow.com, info@seattlemeowtropolitan.com | **Getting there** Bus 44, 62 to N 45th Street & Stone Way N | **Hours** Sun–Mon, Wed–Fri noon–6pm, Tue noon–5pm | **Tip** There are also adoptable cats to hang out with at NEKO, a cat café, that serves wine, beer, sake, coffee, and Japanese snacks (519 E Pine Street, www.nekocatcafe.com/seattle).

85 The Seattle Room

A deep dive into local history

Seattle's downtown Central Public Library building is a striking 11-story polygonal structure designed by architects Rem Koolhaas and Joshua Prince-Ramus and clad in a diamond-shaped pattern of glass and steel. Since opening, in 2004, the building has been a popular destination for both locals and out-of-town visitors, many of whom have little interest in checking out books.

The library's photogenic and oddly shaped building itself is certainly a place you'll want to see. But inside, the 4th or Red Floor, has a circular hallway painted with 13 different shades of red on the walls, ceilings, floors, and stairs. There are meeting rooms on this floor, so it is appropriate that at least one wall bears the text of *Robert's Rules of Order*. In addition to a unique, four-story, walkable spiral of non-fiction book stacks, the building has lots of site-specific public art, including two hidden *trompe-l'oeil* murals – look for an octopus and an astronaut.

The 10th floor offers both a panoramic view out to the city and a perch for looking down through all the building's floors. You might get vertigo or witness a marriage proposal up there, but don't leave without visiting the Seattle Room. This is where you'll be able to see special collections of photographs, postcards, manuscripts, and even restaurant menus and high school yearbooks that tell the story of the city's history and culture.

Library staff fill display cases here with rare documents, ephemera, and other items from the collection to mark historic anniversaries, but Ann Ferguson, Curator of the Special Collections, encourages visitors to make their way to the metal map cases in the back. "The collection includes streetcar maps, maps with mining locations, and other very old maps of Seattle and Washington state," she says, and each day the staff makes a point of setting out an assortment of rare favorites for visitors to see.

Address 1000 4th Avenue, Seattle, WA 98104, +1 (206) 386-4636, www.spl.org | Getting there Bus 2, 12, 15 to 4th Avenue & Madison Street | Hours Sun noon–6pm, Mon–Sat 10am–6pm | Tip The Douglass-Truth Branch of the Seattle Public Library has one of the largest collections of African American literature on the West Coast (2300 E Yesler Way, www.spl.org/hours-and-locations/douglass-truth-branch).

86__Sicks' Stadium Site
Homebase to local baseball history

It is easy to miss the sign marking the "Historic Site of Sick's Stadium" (now Sicks'), outside Lowe's hardware store on Rainier Avenue South. But for more than four decades, the structure that stood here played a key role in Seattle's sports history.

The stadium was built in 1938 by beer magnate Emil G. Sick, then the new owner of the Seattle Rainiers (formerly the Seattle Indians), a minor league team in the Pacific Coast League. One of the team's early stars was a young local pitcher named Fred Hutchinson, who went on to the major leagues as both a player and a manager. The local sports star died of lung cancer in 1964 at age 45. Seattle's Fred Hutchinson Cancer Research Center bears his name today.

The Seattle Rainiers franchise was sold in 1961 to the Boston Red Sox and then to the California Angels, who dubbed the team the Seattle Angels. But Seattle wanted a major league franchise. And when it got one in 1967 from the American League for the Seattle Pilots (sold in 1970 to become the Milwaukee Brewers), the city promised to build a new stadium within 3 years. Sicks' stadium would be replaced by the Kingdome, which was famously imploded in 2000 to make way for a new and improved stadium.

In 1969 Sicks' Stadium hosted the single major league season of the Seattle Pilots. Then, a minor league baseball team, again named the Rainiers, called the stadium home until the mid-1970s. The stadium also hosted concerts, most famously Elvis Presley in 1957 and both Janis Joplin and Jimi Hendrix in 1970. The structure was demolished in 1979 and replaced by a big box hardware store in the 1990s.

Today, there is that *site of* sign out front and, at the store exit, by the hot dog stand, a metal silhouette of a baseball player, a metal home plate, and a sign that reads, in part, *If the year were 1942, you'd be in perfect position to knock one out of the park.*

Address 2700 Rainier Avenue S, Seattle, WA 98144 | Getting there Bus 7 to Rainier Avenue S & S Bayview Street | Hours Unrestricted | Tip Go see *The Mitt*, a 9-foot-tall sculpture by Seattle artist Gerard Tsutakawa and more baseball-themed art at T-Mobile Park, home of the Seattle Mariners (1250 1st Avenue S, www.mlb.com/mariners/ballpark).

87 Silent Reading Party
Mum's the word at Hotel Sorrento

Built in 1909 for the Alaska Yukon Pacific Exposition, the seven-story Hotel Sorrento on First Hill is now one of Seattle's oldest hotels, features Italian Renaissance-style architecture inspired by the storied Excelsior Vittoria hotel in Sorrento, Italy. It is rumored to be haunted by the ghost of Alice B. Toklas, the longtime companion of Gertrude Stein, who was also known for her hash-laced fudge recipe.

Toklas never visited the Hotel Sorrento. But before it was built, a young Toklas and her family lived in a home either on the current hotel site or close by. Perhaps that's why Toklas is said to appear in a white gown in the 4th floor hallway and in room 408. And why "chairs sometimes move, lights turn on and off, and the elevator stops on the 4th floor for no reason," says General Manager Ryan Mac-Donald. The hotel hosts the annual Alice B. Toklas Dinner, inspired by *The Alice B. Toklas Cookbook,* and a Witches' Tea at Halloween.

But every other Wednesday at 6pm, the hotel's octagonal, mahogany-paneled Fireside Room transforms into a Silent Reading Party. During this unusual, oddly intimate, and oh-so-Seattle event, guests bring reading material of their choice and sit quietly on barstools or love seats, at small tables, and in fireside armchairs. You must have a reservation to join in person or on Zoom. Readers listen to live piano music, nibble on meals, and drink themed cocktails with names such as "Romeo and Julep." But the main goal is to read. Alone and yet together.

While most guests arrive with physical books, some bring Kindles, magazines, or newspapers.

"That's fine," says Christopher Frizzelle, the local writer who invented the Silent Reading Party in 2009. "It is a group experience that speaks to the craving people have to tune out Twitter and Facebook for a while and reconnect with the old-fashioned pleasure of reading."

Address 900 Madison Street, Seattle, WA 98104, +1 (206) 622-6400, www.hotelsorrento.com, info@hotelsorrento.com | Getting there Bus 12 to Madison Street & 9th Avenue | Hours Silent Reading Party 6pm every other Wed; lobby unrestricted | Tip Feathers, the taxidermy peacock at the front desk, is from the nearby Frye Art Museum, which presents work by local and global artists free of charge (704 Terry Avenue, www.fryemuseum.org).

88 Sky View Observatory

Locals prefer these sky-high views

Some people get their bearings of a city on a bus tour. Others would rather assess the urban landscape from above. And while Seattle's Space Needle gets plenty of well-deserved love from the "seen from above" crowd for its views, rotating glass floor, and bonus activities, locals often prefer the taller, less expensive, and usually less crowded Sky Observatory on the 73rd floor of the 76-story Columbia Center office tower downtown.

At 902 feet, this is the tallest observatory open to the public in the Pacific Northwest. On clear – and even not so clear – days, you will be rewarded with impressive, 360-degree viewing of Mt. Rainier, the Cascade Mountains, Mt. Baker, Elliott Bay, the Olympic Mountains, the Space Needle, Smith Tower, ferries, and area shipping ports. Exhibits, information panels, and interactive tablets opposite the windows explain exactly what you are seeing, and staff members are happy to answer your questions.

There are plenty of places to take photos or selfies, but two of the best spots are in the northwest and southwest corners, where the windows reach from floor to ceiling. "This is a popular spot for proposals," says the observatory's general manager Edgar Vidal, who also says that many locals in the know head to the observatory for sky high views of downtown events, especially on game days at Lumen Field, home of the Seattle Seahawks football team and the Seattle Sounders soccer team. When the retractable roof is open, T-Mobile Park, home of the Seattle Mariners baseball team, is also in view.

In addition to the observatory café at the top serving cocktails, Northwest beer and wine, espresso drinks, and small meals, there is a gift shop on the atrium level, right by the elevator, which makes the journey up to and down from the 73rd floor in a fast but not too fast 70-second ride, with a free video show about Seattle neighborhoods during the trip.

Address Columbia Center, 700 4th Avenue, Seattle, WA 98104, +1 (206) 386-5564, www.skyviewobservatory.com, news@skyviewobservtory.com | Getting there Bus 1, 2, 3, 4, 5 to 3rd Avenue & James Street; Light Rail to Pioneer Square (1 Line) | Hours Thu–Sun noon–7pm | Tip After seeing the city from above, see it from below on the popular and informative Underground Tour in Pioneer Square (614 1st Avenue, www.undergroundtour.com).

89 __ Smith Tower

Seattle's first skyscraper

When it officially opened on July 4, 1914, the white terracotta-clad Smith Tower in Pioneer Square was the tallest building west of Ohio. High-speed, manually operated Otis elevators whisked tenants to modern offices wired for business with telephone and telegraph outlets and plug-ins for a central vacuum system. For 25 cents, anyone could ride to the 35th floor Chinese Room to see its blackwood furniture and an ornate carved teak ceiling and then step out to the open-air, wraparound observation deck below the building's pyramid-shaped pinnacle. On opening day, 4,200 people visited.

Seattle's first skyscraper was built by east-coast industrialists Lyman Cornelius (L.C.) Smith and his son, Burns Lyman Smith. Their fortune came from typewriters as the "Smith" in what became Smith-Corona, and firearms, although they were *not* the "Smith" in Smith & Wesson. In 1909, L.C. announced plans to build a 14-story office building on land he owned in downtown Seattle. His son convinced him to set his sights much higher. But L.C. died in 1910, leaving Burns to see to completion what was ambitiously advertised as a 42-story building. In fact, there were 36 floors then, and now there are 38.

While no longer the tallest building on the skyline, the renovated Smith Tower still offers an iconic experience. Lobby level exhibits tell of the tower's history and its noted tenants, which included bootleggers and a radio station. A gleaming Otis elevator glides to the 35th floor observatory and the caged, outdoor viewing deck. Inside, the speakeasy-style bar and restaurant retains key Chinese Room elements, most notably the ornate ceiling and the Wishing Chair that, legend has it, assures marriage within a year to unmarried women who sit in it. Enjoy a signature Wishing Chair cocktail (Oola gin, chai-infused Carpano Antica vermouth, and Grand Marnier) and take in the views.

Address 506 2nd Avenue, Seattle, WA 98104, +1 (206) 624-0414, www.smithtower.com, info@smithtower.com | **Getting there** Bus 1, 2, 3, 4, 5 to 3rd Avenue & James Street; Light Rail to Pioneer Square (1 Line) | **Hours** Observatory: Wed, Thu, Sun 11am–8pm, Fri & Sat 11am–9pm (bar opens an hour later) | **Tip** Go see the four-floor parking garage at 2nd Avenue and Yesler Way, known locally as the "Sinking Ship" because its sloping design resembles the bow of a ship.

90_SoDo Track Art

World's longest curated mural corridor

If you usually stare at your phone when riding the bus or light rail, there are more than 50 reasons not to do that when traveling through Seattle's SoDo (South of Downtown) District.

SoDo Track, a public art gallery, is a gift to transit users. Or, as the cultural development agency 4Culture describes it, "an imaginative raceway in motion," in which the gallery rolls horizontally to the viewer.

In a unique public/private partnership, SoDo Track organizers commissioned more than 60 local and international artists to create side-by-side murals along a two-mile stretch of transit corridor that runs through a gritty neighborhood dotted with sports stadiums and warehouses. Blank, transit-facing warehouse walls are the canvases onto which the artists expressed their responses to the common themes of "Motion," "Movement," and "Progress." So, you will see everything from a kaleidoscopic vortex, a sprinting person, and a running cheetah, to a leaping deer, jumping frogs, and encouraging messages such as, "Then Out Came the Sun."

"Most people experience it unplanned on the light rail," says 4Culture's Andy Le. But if you plan your route using the light rail, the bus, and your feet, you can see most of the SoDo Track murals up close and at your leisure.

Christopher Derek Bruno's mural, the bright, multi-hued *Exterior Intervention 1: angle of incidence*" is painted on the corrugated steel rooftop of a building on 6th Avenue S and is best seen from the light rail. Look for it as the train leaves the SoDo Station, heading south toward the Beacon Hill Station. "This project presented the very best kind of challenge an artist could ask for," says Bruno, "a fully supported invitation to push one's abilities, a unique context in which to s-t-r-e-t-c-h out and play, and the chance to affect an unsolicited positive change in the day of another."

Address 5th Avenue S between Royal Brougham Way & Spokane Street, Seattle, www.sodotrack.com | **Getting there** See 35 works along the Light Rail between Stadium & Beacon Hill Stations, 51 murals along Bus 150, 594 through SoDo, and 20 murals along SoDo Trail | **Hours** Unrestricted | **Tip** There is more public art at the Light Rail stations (www.soundtransit.org/system-expansion/creating-vibrant-stations).

91 South Willow Street End

Shoreline access for the rest of us

A benefit of all the bodies of water in and around Seattle, such as Lake Washington, Lake Union, Puget Sound, Elliott Bay, and the Duwamish River, is more than 200 miles of shoreline. Much of that land is privately owned, zoned for commercial or industrial use, or park land. But thanks to a quirk in the way the city developed, there are about 150 streets in Seattle that end right at the water. And the best part is that all those leftover pieces of shoreline are public property.

Locating and accessing these street ends can be challenging though. But thanks to a city council resolution and citizen groups such as the Friends of Street Ends, these slips of shoreline are being steadily reclaimed from weeds and junk piles, and from private citizens who had, over the years, been using the public spaces as their private property. Many of these shoreline street ends have now been mapped, cleaned up, improved, and signed.

In Ballard, for example, the 34th Avenue NW Shoreline Street End has artwork, *A Salish Welcome* by Marvin Oliver, and a great view of the ship canal and the Salmon Bay Bridge.

Across town, there's the S Willow Street site in the Seward Park neighborhood. In 1983, Marty Oppenheimer moved in next door to a then-overgrown and inaccessible shoreline street end on Lake Washington. To the chagrin of some neighbors and to the delight of others, Oppenheimer spearheaded a campaign to clean up the spot for public use.

Today, a wooded path leads from the street down to a waterfront pocket park with two benches under a black locust tree. Rock stairs take you onto a small gravel beach for a free lake view that is the same one the swanky homes nearby have. "While only 40 feet wide, it is picturesque and typically busy with picnickers, stand up paddleboarders, kayakers, and swimmers," says Oppenheimer, "In fact, a couple recently held their wedding here."

Address Next to 5628 S Willow Street, Seattle, WA 98118 | Getting there Bus 50 to Seward Park Avenue S & S Holly Street | Hours Daily dawn–dusk | Tip Visit more shoreline street ends with the help of the Seattle DOT's Shoreline Street Ends Program interactive map (www.seattle.gov/transportation).

92 __ Space Needle Secrets
Fresh views up top, retro souvenirs below

Built for the 1962 Seattle World's Fair, the 605-foot-tall Space Needle remains a top tourist attraction, welcoming more than 1.3 million visitors a year. Seattleites love it too, especially for its New Year's Eve fireworks and the giant flags that appear on the rooftop to salute a local sports team or major event.

But most locals either don't know or don't recall some of the more unusual facts about the oddly shaped landmark. The original 1962 colors were Space Age Astronaut White for the tower, Re-entry Red for the halo, and an orangish Galaxy Gold at the top, befitting the fair's "Century 21" theme. Each night of the fair, a flaming, natural gas torch on top of the Needle lit up in rainbow colors.

And during the Needle's 2017 renovation, when the iconic rotating restaurant was replaced with a unique, rotating glass floor, workers found a forgotten time capsule that should have been opened in 2002, 15 years earlier! Among the many fascinating items that had been placed inside the container were photos from 1962 and 1982, a menu from the original restaurant, and a master key that reportedly opened every lock in the Space Needle in 1982.

The Needle's ground floor gift shop offers a dizzying array of Space Needle-themed souvenirs, but a favorite is the retro Mold-A-Matic machine, delivering plastic models of the Space Needle in 30 seconds. There were six such machines at the 1962 World's Fair, dispensing brightly colored, injection-molded models of the Monorail, the fair's Century 21 logo, the see/hear/speak no evil monkeys, a laughing Buddha figure, or *Hotei*, and, of course, the Space Needle itself. Figures came out warm and smelling like a brand-new box of Crayola crayons, as they still do today. Space Needle officials say their Mold-A-Matic is one of the original machines introduced at the World's Fair but remodeled to include an updated façade and a small TV playing vintage fair footage.

Address 400 Broad Street, Seattle, WA 98109, +1 (206) 905-2100, www.spaceneedle.com, guestservice@spaceneedle.com | Getting there Bus 3, 4 to 5th Avenue N & Broad Street | Hours See website for seasonal hours | Tip Ride the Monorail, another 1962 World's Fair souvenir, between downtown's Westlake Center (5th Avenue & Pine Street) to the Space Needle in 2 minutes. Elvis did it, and you can too (www.seattlemonorail.com).

93 Spice Bridge
Tastes of the world

Arrive hungry at the Spice Bridge Food Hall in the edge city of Tukwila and be ready to try new foods and make some decisions. Eight food vendors, all women of color and immigrants to the region, rotate through the hall's four stalls. They prepare everything in the hall's shared commissary kitchen and offer generously portioned, well-priced food and drink from their homelands.

Depending on which day you visit, the cuisines and countries represented may stretch from Afghanistan, Argentina, and the Congo to Ethiopia, Gambia, and the Philippines. And the menu items offered may include everything from goat stews, *empanadas*, and fish or chicken *yassa* to *alfajores* (Latin American cookie sandwiches), baklava, and *mahamri*, or West African donuts.

While the meals served here are welcome cultural connections for the area's diverse expatriate communities, Spice Bridge also draws foodies, families, and adventurous eaters who appreciate the one-stop concept that encourages ordering a few items from each vendor and then sharing. But this mini-United Nations of food vendors is not only about cooking and eating. A program of Global to Local's Food Innovation Network (FIN), Spice Bridge provides these women with workspaces, and it also helps them learn how to operate and grow their own businesses.

"Some of them may have had a food business before they moved here or were cooking for their families and their neighbors," says Kerrie Carbary, incubator program manager for FIN. Others were making food to sell at weekend farmers markets. Spice Bridge, she explains, offers mentoring and financial assistance, and helps with permits, marketing advice, and more. The goal is for each vendor to build a following, grow their confidence and know-how, and move out into the community as a going concern. So, each time you visit, it might be a whole new world of tastes.

Address Tukwila Village, 14200 Tukwila International Boulevard, Suite 141, Tukwila, WA 98168, +1 (206) 582-1915, www.foodinovationnetwork | Getting there Bus 124 to Tukwila International Boulevard & S 144th Street | Hours Tue–Sat 11am–8pm, Sun 10am–5pm | Tip Visit Highline SeaTac Botanical Garden, where Seike Japanese Garden and Elda Behm's Paradise Garden were moved when SeaTac Airport built a third runway (13735 24th Avenue S, www.highlinegarden.org).

94 The State Hotel

Pike Place Market on the walls

Seattle is blessed with a bevy of charming boutique hotels, each with a unique and sometimes offbeat take on amenities that are often accessible to the public. Case in point: the 91-room State Hotel. "Created to be utterly Seattle," says general manager Rob Nichols.

The State Hotel is located in a historic downtown building that once housed medical offices up above and the landmark Ben Paris Cigars, Lunch & Cards establishment in the basement. Its five-story exterior mural by Shepard Fairey, the street artist best known for creating the Barack Obama *Hope* poster, is the first clue that this hotel is not shy about being eclectic and art-forward. Inside, the lobby has a wall covered in doorknobs. There is a mural in the restaurant by local illustrator and tattoo artist Kyler Martz. And the rooftop deck sports a bright, undulating painting by Takiyah Ward. But Kate Blairstone's flamboyant custom wallpaper collection inspired by Pike Place Market that's featured on the elevator landings offers the most Seattle touch of all.

Hundreds of Blairstone's hand-drawn illustrations of seafood, seasonal produce, fresh flowers, colorful vegetables, odd souvenirs, seagulls, and other images spied at the iconic market can be spotted in the wallcoverings, which are different on each of the hotel's nine floors. "I wanted to highlight the fact that Pike Place has a seasonal aspect to it and is a place with many cultural influences in a concentrated area," says Blairstone. Additionally, Blairstone wanted the artwork to be inclusive of Seattle's street culture, including its grungier attributes. "So, you might see images of Dungeness crab mixed with figs, flowers, and a pressed penny depicting market mascot Rachel the Pig, and then spot a glass pot pipe hidden in there," says Blairstone, "It's got the fish market feel with tasteful Seattle Easter eggs in there to make Seattleites feel seen." Ask the front desk for a floor-by-floor tour.

Address 1501 2nd Avenue, Seattle, WA 98101, +1 (206) 513-7300, www.statehotel.com, info@statehotel.com | Getting there Bus C, D, E 15, 16, 21 to 3rd Avenue & Pike Street; Light Rail to University Street (1 Line) | Hours Unrestricted lobby hours | Tip To see the inspiration for the wallpaper images, walk 99 steps from the hotel's front door to the Pike Place Market entrance (1st Avenue & Pike Street, www.pikeplacemarket.org).

95 Statue of Liberty Plaza

A little Lady Liberty watches over Alki Beach

West Seattle's Alki Beach offers two and a half miles of sand and a walkway that's great for jogging, biking, and taking in views of the Olympic Mountains and all manner of vessels plying across the Puget Sound. As you stroll along, you'll see a series of public artworks, a 2.5-ton anchor discovered by divers, and the *Birthplace of Seattle Monument* (63rd Avenue SW & Alki Avenue SW), which bears the names of the city's first white settlers, who landed on Alki Point on November 13, 1851.

Nearby is another monument that may seem out of place by some 3,000 miles. On a pedestal in a small plaza is a six-foot-tall, 1/18 scale replica of the Statue of Liberty. She arrived here in 1952, a gift from the Boy Scouts of America as part of a nationwide, post-war "Little Sisters of Liberty" campaign that raised enough funds and support to install more than 200 little Lady Liberties in towns across the country. Around 100 remain today.

Seattle's original Lady Liberty had her struggles though. Vandals stole the spikes on her crown and, for a while, her upraised arm was missing as well. Over the years, wind, water, and salty beach air took a structural toll on the statue, which was plaster sheathed in copper. Then, in 2007, a new statue recast in bronze was swapped for the old, and Statue of Liberty Plaza remains a powerful symbol in this community gathering spot. If you'd like to see the original statue, just walk a few blocks to the Log House Museum at 3003 61st Avenue SW which is operated by the Southwest Seattle Historical Society. You can see it through a window in the museum's annex.

"A lot of work needs to be done refurbishing and restoring the old statue," says former historical society executive director Michal King. "It's a prized element of our collection. But we think to appreciate one you have to see both. Together they speak to a longer story."

Address Statue of Liberty Plaza, Alki Avenue SW & 61st Avenue SW, Seattle, WA 98116 | **Getting there** Bus 50, 56, 775 to Alki Avenue SW & 61st Avenue SW | **Hours** Unrestricted | **Tip** Built by one of Seattle's founders, Dr. David Swinson "Doc" Maynard, the house considered to be Seattle's oldest was built in the late 1850s or early 1860s (3045 64th Avenue SW).

96_ Streissguth Garden

Lush hillside with a fairytale story

With 293 steps, Blaine Street Steps is Seattle's second longest stairway. Howe Street Stairs' 388 steps make it the longest. Both are popular for casual walks and workouts, but there is a hidden treasure near the top of the Blaine Street Steps, and that's Streissguth Gardens, an urban oasis with intertwining paths, sweeping views of Lake Union and the Olympics Mountains, and a charming creation story.

In the 1960s, love bloomed when Daniel Streissguth and his next-door neighbor on the Blaine Street Steps, Ann Pytkowicz, each set about transforming the steep hillside behind their homes into terraced gardens. They married in 1968, moving into the light-filled home that Dan, an architect, had built beside the stair. A few years later, the couple bought two empty, overgrown lots across the stair from their home. After discovering native trillium on the land and creating a path to it, they began gardening these lots in earnest, carving out a hillside garden with paths, benches, and pleasing patches of Northwest native plants around each bend. In 1996, the plots were gifted to the city so that they, along with some adjacent land condo developers had their sights on, could become part of the city's greenbelt. Today, Seattle Parks and Recreation is the official landowner, but the family actively maintains Streissguth Gardens.

Dan Streissguth died in 2020 at age 96. But love continues to grow in the garden, as their son Ben Streissguth, now the garden manager, met his wife, Jade Takashima, while giving a garden tour. Now the couple works together as a team to care for, manage, and plan the historic preservation of the fairytale garden.

The one-acre public garden area on the south side of the Blaine Street stair is open to the public for free. Tours of the Streissguth's private garden on the north side of the stairs are available by appointment.

Address 1640 Broadway E, Seattle, WA 98102, +1 (206) 280-5842, streissguthgardens.com, ben@streissguthgardens.com | Getting there Bus 49 to 10th Avenue E & E Howe Street | Hours Unrestricted | Tip Ben and Jade urge garden lovers to visit the Good Shepherd Center's grounds in Wallingford to see many exotic plant specimens and a century-old apple orchard (4649 Sunnyside Avenue N, www.historicseattle.org/project/good-shepherd).

97___Suzzallo Library

Hogwarts or the University of Washington?

Harry Potter fans, architecture aficionados, and bibliophiles must visit the University of Washington's Suzzallo Library, which students dubbed a "cathedral of books" at its opening in 1927. Reading room experts ranked this library one of the most beautiful in the world.

Designed in the collegiate gothic style by Seattle architects Carl Gould, Sr. and Charles Bebb, creators of the 1915 campus plan, the library was intended to be "the soul of the university," according to university president and library namesake, Henry Suzzallo.

Without touching a book, you can learn a lot from "reading" the building itself. Above the grand main doors, the three cast-stone figures by Tacoma sculptor Allan Clark symbolize "Mastery," "Inspiration," and "Thought." The subjects for the 18 terracotta figures in the exterior niches, also made by Clark, were drawn from a faculty-suggested line-up of the world's most important thinkers and doers. The line-up includes notables, such as Louis Pasteur, Shakespeare, Plato, Benjamin Franklin, Sir Isaac Newton, Leonardo da Vinci, Galileo, and others, though, notably, none are women.

Step inside the building and walk up the curving, grand staircase to the Reading Room, the Hogwarts-like, vaulted-ceiling celebrity of the facility. 65 feet high, 52 feet wide and 250 feet long, the room is filled with long, oak study tables topped by brass lamps. Lighted, hand-painted globes hanging at each end of the room bear the names of Leif Erickson, Marco Polo, Columbus, Magellan, and other explorers.

Other spare-no-detail touches include oak bookcases topped by ornamental friezes with carvings of plants, flowers, and trees native to our state, and a series of stained and leaded glass windows adorned with watermarks used by papermakers working in the late Middle Ages and early Renaissance, without whom we might not have so many library-worthy books.

Address Red Square, University of Washington Campus, 1840 NE Grant Lane, Seattle, WA 98195, +1 (206) 543-0242, www.lib.washington.edu/suzzallo | Getting there Light Rail to U District (1 Line); bus 70 to 15th Avenue E & NE Campus Parkway | Hours Mon–Thu 9am–8pm, Fri 9am–5pm, Sun 1–8pm | Tip Take a self-guided tour of more than two dozen outdoor artworks on the UW campus (www.facilities.uw.edu/files/media/campus-art-collection-tour.pdf).

98__Ted Bundy's Dormitory

A serial killer slept in McMahon Hall

In an episode of his CNN series, *Parts Unknown*, filmed in Seattle in late 2017, the late chef and culture connoisseur Anthony Bourdain asks locals why so many serial killers hail from Seattle and the Pacific Northwest. "You can hide bodies a short distance from wherever you are," quips journalist and author Knute Berger. Or maybe it's the long, gray, and rainy winters. Whatever the reason, there have indeed been several notorious serial killers from the region.

Gary Ridgway, a Seattle-area truck painter dubbed the Green River Killer, was convicted in 2003 of strangling and murdering almost 50 young women during the 1980s and 90s. He later admitted to killing dozens more. Many of his victims were prostitutes and teenage runaways who Ridgway thought no one would ever miss. He would dump their bodies in or near the banks of the Green River, along freeways, or in remote wooded areas. He is currently serving a life sentence with no option for parole.

Before Ridgway, though, there was Ted Bundy, one of the most infamous serial killers of all time. Raised in Tacoma and a graduate of the University of Washington, in the 1970s Bundy murdered more than 30 women – possibly up to 100 – in and around Seattle and other parts of Washington, as well as in Oregon, California, Colorado, Florida, Idaho, and Utah. Described as handsome and charming, Bundy was said to have lured many of his victims into his Volkswagen car and to their gruesome deaths by impersonating authority figures or pretending to be injured and in need of help. In 1989, Bundy was executed in the electric chair in Florida.

Ted Bundy attended the University of Washington – twice. He enrolled in 1966, dropped out, and came back to earn his psychology degree in 1972. In 1966, perhaps before he became a murderer who strangled and sometimes decapitated his victims, he lived on campus in McMahon Hall.

Address McMahon Hall, University of Washington campus, 4200 Whitman Court NE, Seattle, WA 98195 | **Getting there** Bus 75, 372 to Stevens Way & Pend Oreille Road; Light Rail to U District (1 Line) | **Hours** Unrestricted from the outside only | **Tip** The Jacob Lawrence Gallery in the Art Building hosts a dozen exhibitions a year (1915 NE Chelan Lane, Room 132, www.art.washington.edu/jacob-lawrence-gallery).

99__Two Big Blondes
Oldest, largest, plus-size resale store

Opened in 1997 by, you guessed it, two big blondes, Two Big Blondes (TBB) is likely the oldest and, at 4,000 square feet, arguably the largest plus-size resale store in the country. Now owned by Lisa Michaud, a big brunette, this Central District shop stocks clothing sizes 14 and larger, shoes in size 8 and up, and accessories galore. TBB is a destination for a growing circle of regulars, who come from all over to find clothes they'll love.

"Thrift stores and other consignment shops might have a small section of women's plus-sized clothing, but many first-time customers often cry because it's not just that we have plus sizes, it's the volume – about 10,000 items – the quality, and the variety we have," says Michaud.

TBB has all kinds of clothing for all kinds of styles, including comfortable and casual, vintage, high-end designer pieces, and swimwear. It's all second-hand and on consignment, but some items come in new with tags. Occasionally, TBB features clothing from one plus-size celebrity consigner, Seattle's Lindy West, author of *Shrill: Notes from a Loud Woman*, which was turned into a TV series.

Michaud says the store's clientele is diverse and includes anyone who wants to wear women's clothing, as well as people with different feelings about their bodies as plus-sized. "Some people are very comfortable and ready to wear anything," says Michaud. "Some trans women don't feel they have safe places to shop or are learning what clothing and shoes will fit them. And other people just have a really hard time and are used to covering up their bodies. So, we are happy to help people find clothes that make them feel good and look great."

Two Big Blondes contributes clothes that are donated and items that remain unsold after consignment to a local non-profit organization that provides clothing to local area residents who are experiencing economic difficulties or homelessness.

Address 2501 S Jackson Street, Seattle, WA 98144, +1 (206) 762-8620,
www.twobigblondes.com, info@twobigblondes.com | Getting there Bus 8, 14 to
23rd Avenue S & S Jackson Street | Hours Tue–Sat 11am–6pm | Tip Jackson's Catfish
Corner down the street serves signature catfish, prawns, hush puppies, and other sides
(2218 S Jackson Street, www.jacksonscatfishcorner.com).

100 _ Unicorn & Narwhal

Colorful and conjoined carnival-themed bars

If you're looking for a cozy little bar on Capitol Hill, where you can order a one-off, mixologist-concocted cocktail and settle in for a quiet conversation, then steer clear of the two-in-one Unicorn & Narwhal bars. But if a boozy, wacky, theme-bar adventure is in the cards, this is the place to go.

The décor is a colorful, kitschy cacophony of taxidermy trophies, bright stripes, and intricately painted circus and salvaged cast-offs that artistic mastermind and venue co-owner Adam Heimstadt describes as his own "carnival/tattoo take on new American folk art." Hard to describe and impossible to forget, the two bars Heimstadt painstakingly put together, Unicorn up above and Narwhal carved out of the basement below, create a space so garishly welcoming that, in 2015, Seattle-born rapper Macklemore and Ryan Lewis filmed scenes here for their wildly popular "Thrift Shop" music video, which now has more than a billion views. Fans can take selfies under a sign in Narwhal marking *The Unremarkable Spot Where Macklemore Stood*.

At both bars, the drink menus lean heavily to Jell-O shots and sugary, "magical" cocktails, with names like My Little Pony, The Mystical Mermaid, and Unicorn Jizz. Carnival food, including corn dogs, funnel cakes, fried ice-cream, and Unicorn Balls (fried pork balls), provides sustenance and may help soak up the booze. For entertainment, there's karaoke, trivia, drag queen bingo, and a Sunday drag brunch. And for sport, the array of arcade games downstairs in the Narwhal bar includes Skee-Ball, classic pinball machines, and a vintage claw machine that rewards players with stuffed animals and, for the lucky ones, sex toys.

Weekend nights can be raucous, but if you stop in during the afternoon or early evening, you'll be able to leisurely tour and enjoy Heimstadt's bar-wide artwork and have your pick of arcade games to play.

Address 1118 E Pike Street, Seattle, WA 98122, +1 (206) 325-6492, www.unicornseattle.com | Getting there Light Rail to Capitol Hill (1 Line); First Hill Streetcar to Broadway & Pike | Hours Unicorn: Mon–Fri 2pm–1:45am, Sat & Sun 11am–1:45am; Narwhal: Mon–Thu 6pm–1:45am, Fri–Sun 4pm–1:45am | Tip Head over to nearby Ox Billiards, an all-ages pool hall with loads of snooker and pool tables, plus lessons (1432 Broadway, www.oxbilliards.com).

101 Volunteer Park Conservatory

Horticultural Heaven

Volunteer Park Conservatory Senior Gardener David Helgeson clearly enjoys showing visitors through the Victorian-style greenhouse built in 1912 from a prefabricated kit that came with 3,426 glass panes. Inside is an oasis that includes rare specimens, a signature orchid collection, plants over 100 years old, and some that are carnivorous. But Helgeson says two non-plant building features that delight him are often overlooked.

One is the peacock window over the front door that is the only piece of original glass and wood remaining from the original 1912 structure after two renovations. The other is the artwork over the entryway created by Richard Spaulding in 1981. *Homage in Green* is a stunning, rectangular, hand-blown, stained-glass canopy that has a painted and etched border containing ornamental botanical designs spanning 300 years.

Inside the conservatory are five rooms: the Palm House, home to a rare, 25-foot-tall bird of paradise; the Cactus House; the Fern House; the Bromeliad House; and the Seasonal Display House, used to showcase everything from azaleas and flowering bulbs to hydrangeas and chrysanthemums. Come winter, a holiday express train winds its way through the poinsettias. And Santa arrives! "We think of it as a museum that has artwork that is living," says Helgeson.

The conservatory's insectivorous plants, which include Venus fly traps, sundews, and American pitcher plants, such as cobra lilies, are very popular with visitors. "We make sure docents always have a stash of wriggly mealworms to feed these plants," says Helgeson. "It grosses some people out, but kids really love it, and it is a great way to start a discussion about plants." And to explain that it can take up to two weeks for these carnivorous plants to digest an entire mealworm.

Address 1400 E Galer Street, Seattle, WA 98112, +1 (206) 684-4743, www.volunteerparkconservatory.org, foc@volunteerparkconservatory.org | Getting there Bus 49 to 10 Avenue E & E Galer Street, or bus 10 to 15th Avenue E & E Galer Street | Hours Tue–Sun 10am–4pm | Tip Volunteer Park Water Tower sits on top of Capitol Hill and has interior spiral stairways that lead to a viewing platform with free views of Seattle and the surrounding landscape (1247 15th Avenue E, www.seattle.gov/parks/find/parks/volunteer-park).

102 Waterfall Garden Park

Pocket park marks the birthplace of UPS

A hidden oasis with a waterfall and lush plantings in the historic Pioneer Square neighborhood marks the birthplace of the modern-day delivery company we know as the United Parcel Service, or UPS.

In 1907, two entrepreneurial teenagers, James Casey and Claude Ryan, borrowed $100 to set up the American Messenger Company. Their office was in a basement below a noisy saloon owned by Ryan's uncle, and their team of teenaged messengers raced around Seattle, delivering notes and running errands by foot and bicycle, and, later, by trolley. The advent of the telephone made messenger services old hat, so the company smartly pivoted to delivering commercial packages by motorcycle and, with the purchase of a converted Ford Model T in 1913, by truck.

UPS grew and prospered, and later its headquarters moved out of Seattle, first to New York, then to Connecticut and, eventually to Georgia. The company is now a powerhouse in trucking, air freight, and retail shipping, as well as finance and international trade services.

The UPS link to Seattle, however, is not forgotten. The public Waterfall Garden Park now sits on the half-acre spot where the original UPS headquarters was once located. It was built in 1977 by the Annie E. Casey Foundation, named for founder James Casey's mother, and rededicated on August 28, 2007, on the 100th anniversary of the company's founding. The gated, L-shaped, vest-pocket park is 60 by 80 feet and has a well-maintained terraced patio filled with lush plants and seasonal flowers. A refreshing, fast-flowing, 22-foot waterfall cascades 5,000 gallons of filtered and recirculated water per minute onto granite boulders.

Benches and small tables with chairs invite you to linger with a coffee, lunch, a book, or a mobile gadget on which you can make an online order for something that will arrive at your house on one of those brown UPS trucks.

Address 219 2nd Avenue S, Seattle, WA 98104, +1 (206) 838-2266, www.pioneersquare.org | Getting there Bus 1, 2, 4, 7 to 3rd Avenue S & S Main Street; Light Rail to Pioneer Square (1 Line); First Hill Streetcar to Occidental Mall / Pioneer Square | Hours Sun–Sat 8am–3:45pm | Tip Stop for a coffee or a snack in nearby Occidental Square, with play areas, woodcarvings, and frequent outdoor art events (117 S Washington Street, www.seattle.gov/parks/find/parks/occidental-square).

103 Wedgwood Rock

Giant geological souvenir and local landmark

In most any other neighborhood, it would have been dynamited to make room for more homes and wider sidewalks. But the huge boulder once known as Lone Rock, then Big Rock, and now Wedgwood Rock has been on this spot for thousands of years.

At 19 feet tall, 80 feet around, and weighing in at about 1.5 million pounds, the rock certainly stands out for its enormous and imposing size. How did it get here? Geologists say a glacier passed through the area 15 to 20,000 years ago and left the rock behind. They add that it is technically an "erratic boulder" because it does not match the rock types in the area.

Native Americans who first lived in this region knew this rock well and used it as a forest landmark. Later, when the rock sat on the outskirts of the city, Seattle residents would plan picnic outings beside it. Climbers, including Boy Scouts and noted Mountaineers, used the rural rock for practice. In the early 1940s, land around the rock was sold to a developer, who planned a neighborhood of modest homes and was convinced to leave the rock in place. The big boulder became a popular community gathering spot. So popular that in 1970, after some neighbors complained to the city council about "hippies" and raucous climbers frequenting the site day and night, an ordinance was passed making it "unlawful for anyone to climb or be upon that certain rock or boulder known as the Wedgwood Rock," punishable by a fine of up to $100.

Today, Wedgwood Rock remains an odd but much-loved local landmark that sits surrounded by trees on the parking strip between two homes. There are no signs identifying the big boulder or noting its geological significance. But Wedgwood Rock does get a 4.5-star rating on Yelp. And its protectors in the neighborhood say visitors come by to take selfies and, despite the "stay off the rock" law still on the books, occasionally go for a climb.

Address Northwest 72nd Street & 28th Avenue NE, Seattle, WA 98115 | **Getting there** Bus 79, 372 to 25th Avenue NE & NE 75th Street | **Hours** Unrestricted | **Tip** For a totally legal climb, head to the UW Rock on the University of Washington campus, with five outdoor walls offering challenges ranging from novice to expert (3800 Montlake Boulevard NE).

104 West Boston Staircase
19 scary steps

It is not the oldest public stairway in the city. Nor is it the longest or the prettiest. In fact, once you locate what is left of the West Boston staircase on steep and stairway-rich Queen Anne Hill, it will look quite unimpressive. But of the more than 500 staircases the Seattle Department of Transportation maintains, and the 60 or so sets looked after by Seattle Parks and Recreation, these are the only public stairs in Seattle that are said to be haunted.

As legend has it, sometime in the early 1900s, a young man and a young woman who were engaged to be married were climbing up the wooden staircase along the hillside at this spot. The day was sunny, but there had been a great deal of rain in the days before. The man got to the top of the stairs first, but his lovely fiancé stood for a moment on a landing, looking up at her intended. Suddenly, she was swept to her death when the lower portion of the stairs fell away in a landslide.

Sad, right? But here is where the haunting comes in. Many years later, in the late 1980s, a woman named Judy is starting down the new sturdier, concrete staircase that was built to replace the wooden set. "Stop," says a woman's voice, "Don't go any further." Judy stops. (Wouldn't you?) She looks around but sees no one. Then the staircase below where she is standing falls away in a landslide, leaving just 19 steps behind.

Thomas Horton, an architect who walked and then mapped the more than 120 public stairways on Queen Anne Hill, says he learned the details of the haunted stairway while there documenting the staircase for his project. "A neighbor came out to tell me the story," says Horton. But it was not until later, when he was telling the story to the neighborhood newspaper, "that it occurred to me that the woman who told me the story was the right age to have been Judy herself. And that creeped me out."

Address The West Boston staircase is to the left of the house at 2201 11th Avenue W, Seattle, WA 98119 | Getting there Bus 1 to 10th Avenue W & W McGraw Street | Hours Unrestricted | Tip With artistic brickwork, decorative arches, and views of the Olympic Mountains, the crisscrossing stairs along the retaining wall locals call the Wilcox Walls offer an unhaunted West Queen Anne walk (8th Avenue W and 8th Place W).

105__The Wildrose

One of the last lesbian bars

The Wildrose opened on New Year's Eve in 1984, ushering in 1985 with a lesbian bar for Seattle that is now a Capitol Hill cultural institution and one of just a handful of lesbian bars left in the nation. "We believe we're also the oldest lesbian bar in the country," says Shelley Brothers, who used to frequent the bar and has co-owned it with Martha Manning since 2005. Before 1985, there had, of course, been bars in the city that welcomed the lesbian and gay communities. But the Wildrose was the first bar in town to proudly proclaim itself a place where lesbians were welcome to gather, have fun, and be safe.

Over 37 years, "The Rose" has evolved with the neighborhood and lesbian culture itself. Once only women were allowed in the door. Now, the bar is more inclusive. Brothers says she and Manning have faced quite a bit of discrimination in their lives, "And we don't want anyone else to go through that." She notes that these days, a lot of the bar's customers identify as non-binary rather than lesbian. "And we don't want to exclude them. We also all have straight friends that like to go out with us. So, our main concern is that everyone in the bar respects each other. If there are any problems whatsoever, though, we are right on top of it."

The Wildrose has big windows that look out on Pike Street, several blocks of which The Rose takes over during three days of Seattle Pride in June. Year-round inside the bar, activities range from live bands, karaoke, and weekend DJs to drag shows, burlesque, and open mics. "We try to present diverse programming that gives a stage to people that might not normally get a stage," says Brothers. Sports fans are welcome too, when the Wildrose tunes the TVs to The Storm, Seattle's WNBA team; OL Reign, Tacoma's professional women's soccer team; Seattle Seahawks football; and, if they're on a winning streak, Mariners baseball games.

Address 1021 E Pike Street, Seattle, WA 98122, +1 (206) 324-9210,
www.thewildrosebar.com, info@thewildrosebar.com | Getting there Bus 11 to E Pine Street
& 12th Avenue; First Hill Streetcar to Broadway & Pike | Hours Tue & Thu 5–10pm,
Fri & Sat 5pm–midnight, Sun 3–7pm | Tip A branch of the non-profit Out of the Closet
Thrift Store is across the street. Proceeds fund AIDS Healthcare Foundation's HIV/AIDS
programs (1016 E Pike Street, www.outofthecloset.org).

106___Wing Luke Museum
The Asian Pacific American experience

Look up as you step into the lobby of the Wing Luke Museum in the Chinatown-International District to see *Sweet Hello*, Saya Moriyasu's colorful, chandelier-like sculpture decorated with 108 bells. The work's assortment of small faces is meant to represent and welcome many of the Asian communities whose stories the museum tells. And take a seat on the bench in the second floor light well, which was once part of the hotel on this site that housed Asian immigrants. There, in *Letter Cloud*, by Susie Kozawa and Erin Shie Palmer, you'll see copies of many poignant letters those immigrants sent home. You'll hear the letters read both in their native languages and in translation.

Elsewhere in the building, you'll encounter temporary and permanent exhibitions exploring everything from the Pan-Asian Pacific American immigrant and refugee experience to the life of martial arts legend Bruce Lee. Lee lived in Seattle for several formative years and is buried alongside his son, Brandon, in Lake View Cemetery on Capitol Hill (see ch. 61). An installment of the ongoing *Do You Know Bruce?* exhibit series is on the museum's first floor, and do not miss the *Green Hornet & Kato* display tucked into the third-floor landing. Lee played the Green Hornet's masked sidekick, Kato, on a TV show that ran for one season (1966–1967). The museum displays a selection of rare, show-branded toys, including a Halloween costume, walkie talkies, a kite, and a lunchbox from local collector Perry Lee's collection.

Museum admission includes a tour of the building's historic spaces, including the adjacent Yick Fung Co. Chinese import store and, up above, the Gee How Oak Tin Association Hall that welcomed new immigrants to the International District. For a small extra charge, you can also join one of the museum's excellent guided neighborhood tours themed to food, architecture, history, and heritage.

Address 719 S King Street, Seattle, WA 98104, +1 (206) 623-5124, www.wingluke.org, visit@wingluke.org | Getting there Bus 7, 14, 36 to S Jackson Street & 8th Avenue S; Light Rail to International District/Chinatown (1 Line); First Hill Streetcar to 7th & Jackson/Chinatown | Hours Wed–Sun 10am–5pm | Tip While in the International District, visit Maneki, a Japanese restaurant dating back to 1904 that is said to be the first place in Seattle to serve sushi (304 6th Avenue S, www.manekiseattle.com).

107 __ Wonderful Whirligigs

Artistic energy transforms electric substation

Electrical substations are usually unwelcome neighborhood eyesores. But thanks to a team of artists and more than two dozen "whirligigs," or quirky windmills, what could have been an ugly corner has green park space and lots of art instead.

In the late 1970s, as one of the earliest examples of artists working with architects from the start of a public project, artists Andrew Keating, Sherry Markovitz, and Buster Simpson were invited to add color and whimsy to the transformers and other electrical generating equipment at the Viewland-Hoffman Electrical Substation in North Seattle. The team also used some of its project funding to purchase and install 27 whirligigs made by Emil Gehrke and his wife Stella Veva Gehrke.

The Gehrkes, who lived in eastern Washington, near Grand Coulee, were well-known for filling their yard – and the yards of others – with their colorful, spinning, folk art creations made from scavenged and recycled items. Their whirligigs and carousels cleverly make use of everything from chandeliers sections and washing machine parts to broken toys, multi-sized funnels, bicycle wheels, slotted spoons, frying pans, and all manner of discarded utensils, tools, and other treasures they'd pluck from other people's discard piles. In their basement, Emil would make the windmills, and then Stella would paint them. At the Viewland-Hoffman electrical substation, the Gehrkes' handiwork now spins and entertains from inside a specially made, walk-through whirligig compound that protects the art while allowing viewing from multiple angles.

Out in Grand Coulee, 233 miles from Seattle, Gehrke Windmill Garden at North Dam Park displays about 100 of the couple's creations and is on the Washington Heritage Register of Historic Places. The trip out is worth it, but those who do not want to make the almost four-hour trek can enjoy the Gehrkes' handiwork in town.

Address 10533 Fremont Avenue N, Seattle, WA 98133 | Getting there Bus 40 to N 105th Street & Fremont Avenue N | Hours Unrestricted | Tip Just north of the substation is an entry point to the Interurban Trail North for biking, hiking, walking, and some fun, flip book-style artwork (N 110th Street just east of Fremont Avenue N).

108_ Woodland Park Zoo
Gorillas and why zoos now have natural settings

In the 1950s and 1960s, a western lowland gorilla named Bobo moved into Seattle's 92-acre Woodland Park Zoo and became "the toast of the town," according to former zoo director David Towne. An Anacortes family had purchased Bobo as a baby to raise, but they sold him to the zoo when he grew too large. For many years after his death in 1968, fans could visit a taxidermy Bobo at the Museum of History and Industry. The zoo's next generation of gorillas also became famous. But this time, it was for the way they were exhibited.

Most zoos built before the 1960s housed animals in cramped cages with concrete floors. But in 1979, the Woodland Park Zoo kicked off a revolution in zoo design by being the first to build immersion habitats, transforming sterile exhibits into open spaces with lush settings that stimulate natural animal behavior, such as foraging, socializing, and breeding. "There are no chain link barriers," says Towne, "The grounds are planted to reflect nature. And to visitors, it looks like the animals can just walk out."

The concept, created by Seattle-based Jones & Jones architects and landscape designers, was first used to create a new home for Pete, Nina, and Kiki, gorillas who had lived at the zoo since the late 1960s. "Nina, the older female, was the first to venture in," says Towne. "The two big, tough males let her lead the way." Propping up a broken tree limb, clever Kiki was the first – and last – gorilla to venture out. "David Hancocks, the director at the time, tried explaining to the person who reported the escape that it just looked like that because of all the natural plantings. But the person pointed out that the gorilla was sitting on a bend in the public pathway."

Today, the zoo has one of the most successful gorilla programs, with a multi-generational gorilla family that roams freely through two secure, lush environments.

Address 5500 Phinney Avenue N, Seattle, WA 98103, +1 (206) 548-2500, www.zoo.org, zooinfo@zoo.org | Getting there Bus 5, 16 to Phinney Avenue N & N 55th Street | Hours See website for seasonal hours | Tip Zoo animals snack on spent flowers from the Woodland Park Rose Garden. You may stroll through the park, but no snacking (750 N. 50th Street, www.zoo.org/roses).

109 __ Woody Guthrie's Legacy
A fascist-killing guitar at MoPOP

MoPOP was founded as the Experience Music Project by the late Microsoft cofounder Paul Allen and rebranded as the Museum of Pop Culture to reflect a broadened focus. Here, the guitar is a big deal, with more than 300 in MoPOP's collection. And in separate exhibits you'll find the Fender Stratocaster Jimi Hendrix played at Woodstock in 1969 and the first guitar Nirvana's Kurt Cobain smashed.

In a dedicated Guitar Gallery, about 17 guitars linked to iconic musicians tell the story of how the electric and acoustic guitars shaped popular music. Among them is a guitar that once belonged to Woody Guthrie, who penned "This Land is Your Land" and more than 1,000 other songs. The iconic folk musician and political activist spent time in the Pacific Northwest, most notably in the spring of 1941 when the Bonneville Power Administration (BPA) hired him to write songs promoting the benefits of cheap hydroelectric power and the Grand Coulee Dam. Guthrie wrote 26 songs during this one-month gig, including "Roll On Columbia," which became the official folk song of Washington state in 1987.

Guthrie was known for playing guitars bearing a drawing, etching, or sticker with the anti-totalitarian motto, "This Machine Kills Fascists." Hitler was Guthrie's first target, but later the phrase was redirected at the evils embodied by all manner of oppressive powers-that-be.

According to Jacob McMurray, Director of Curatorial, Collections & Exhibits at MoPOP, "Sometime in the late 1930s, Guthrie carved the swaggering threat, along with his name, into the back of the worn 1936 Martin 000-18 we have on display. This makes it the first known instrument to bear the slogan." McMurray says the words on the guitar are very faint. But because guitars in this exhibit are displayed vertically, visitors are able to get within an inch of the instrument and see Guthrie's etching.

Address 325 5th Avenue N, Seattle, WA 98109, +1 (206) 770-2700, www.mopop.org, info@mopop.org | Getting there Seattle Center Monorail to Seattle Center | Hours Sun–Tue & Thu–Sat 10am–5pm | Tip The Crocodile, the storied Belltown club where Nirvana, Pearl Jam, and other iconic local bands performed, is still around, but in a new location (2505 1st Avenue, www.thecrocodile.com).

110_ World Flight Monument

The first round-the-world flight started here

The 350-acre Warren G. Magnuson Park sits on a mile-long stretch of Lake Washington shoreline and is a popular spot for hiking, boating, swimming, kite-flying, and more. But long before it became the city's second-largest park, this prime piece of real estate on the Sand Point peninsula in northeast Seattle was a military base, Sand Point Naval Air Station, and a spot where early aviation history was made.

On April 6, 1924, four US Army Douglas World Cruisers, each with two crewmembers, took off from what was then Sand Point Airfield. Their goal: Complete the first circumnavigation of the globe by air. The four planes were named *Seattle*, *Chicago*, *Boston*, and *New Orleans*. Due to weight restrictions, no more than 300 pounds of supplies were loaded into each open-cockpit plane. The decision was made to leave some equipment, including parachutes and life preservers, behind.

The journey was far from easy. On their way around the world, the teams encountered freezing temperatures, typhoons, mechanical breakdowns, crashes, and other obstacles. But on September 28, 1924, despite losing two of the original four planes, the *Chicago*, the *New Orleans*, and the *Boston II* (a replacement) landed back at Sand Point. The journey had taken 175 days, the crew had made 74 stops, and the team had covered about 27,550 miles.

Today, that first flight around the world is marked with a concrete pillar on a small island at the entrance of the former Naval air station. At the top of the pillar is a large pair of bird wings. At the bottom, a plaque with dates of the flight and the names of the crewmen and their planes.

Inside the park, visitors will find the Air, Land and Sea Playground, which includes several features that give a nod to the site's past as an airfield, including a central sidewalk with markings at each end – an homage to the runway that was once there.

Address 7400 Sand Point Way NE, Seattle, WA 98115, +1 (206) 684-4946, www.seattle.gov/
parks/find/parks/magnuson-park | **Getting there** Bus 62, 75 to Sand Point Way NE &
NE 74th Street | **Hours** Unrestricted | **Tip** One of six sculptures on the adjacent NOAA
campus is *A Sound Garden*, by Douglas Hollis, which emits wind-driven sounds and is the
namesake of Seattle rock band Soundgarden (7600 Sand Point Way NE, www.wrc.noaa.gov).

111 Ye Olde Curiosity Shop

Century-old shrine to the world's oddest wonders

Technically, it is a souvenir shop that has been selling trinkets since 1899. But to generations of locals and visitors alike, Ye Olde Curiosity Shop is a wonderful, jumbly odditorium, literally filled to the rafters with very unusual objects, from whale penises and a trio of human mummies, to miniature carved wonders and mysterious creatures plucked from the sea.

The store is named after Charles Dickens' novel *The Old Curiosity Shop* and was the brainchild of Joseph Edward "Daddy" Standley. He turned a childhood love of anthropology and curious objects into a profitable business and tourist attraction on Seattle's waterfront by sourcing treasures from Alaskan explorers, Native Americans, and world travelers. Over the years, several generations of Standley's family joined the team, moved the store a few times, and added many more strange and startling curiosities to the collection, including two-headed calves, a two-faced cat, a Feejee Mermaid, and a 67-pound snail.

Ask the staff about their favorite objects. Receiving manager Jennifer Mills is partial to the store's collection of more than a dozen shrunken heads and the jar labeled "Freak Pig" that contains a pickled piglet born in 1944 with eight legs, three eyes, two tails, and two noses – it lived for just a few hours. Curio wrangler Peg Boettcher adores the four-legged taxidermy chicken. "I find her life inspiring," she says. "Despite the challenge of having a pair of extra legs, she lived a long and happy, normal chicken life as a barnyard denizen and layer of eggs."

And Andy James, great-grandson of Joseph Edward Standley and current shop owner, remains charmed by some of the wee things displayed in the miniatures case, including the dressed fleas, the tiny figures inside walnut shells, and the images of Mount Rushmore and The Last Supper painted on pinheads.

Address Pier 54, 1001 Alaskan Way, Seattle, WA 98104, +1 (206) 682-5844, www.facebook.com/YeOldeCuriosity, oldecuriosityshop@yahoo.com | Getting there Bus 120, 125 to Columbia Street & Alaskan Way | Hours See website | Tip Ivar's Acres of Clams, the flagship location of 'flounder' Ivar Haglund's chain of seafood bars and restaurants, is also on Pier 54 with al fresco dining and great Elliott Bay views (1001 Alaskan Way, www.ivars.com/acres).

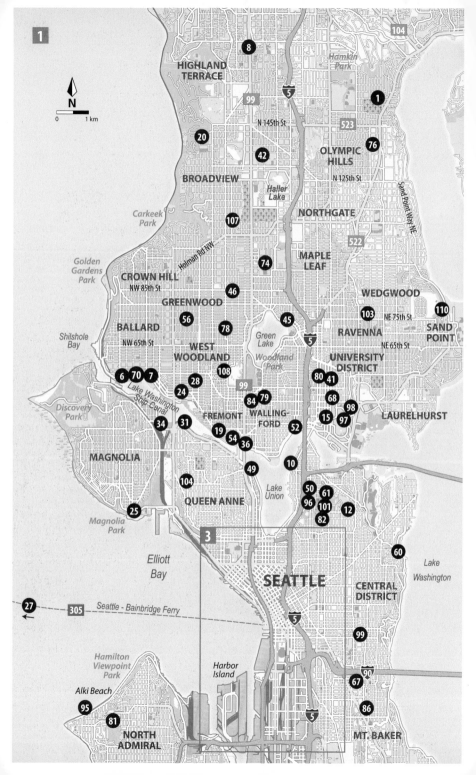

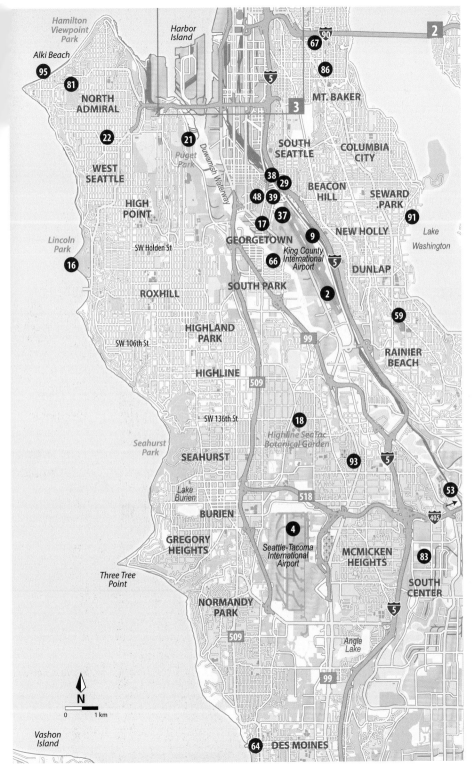

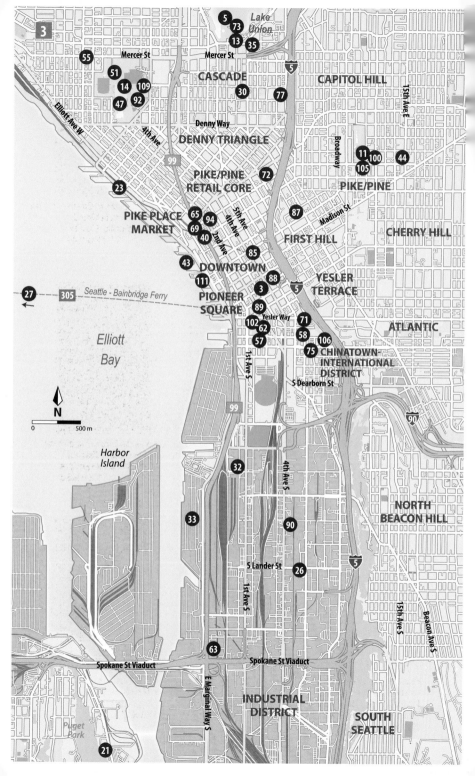

Katrina Nattress, Jason Quigley
**111 Places in Portland
That You Must Not Miss**
ISBN 978-3-7408-0750-4

David Doroghy, Graeme Menzies
**111 Places in Vancouver
That You Must Not Miss**
ISBN 978-3-7408-0494-7

David Doroghy, Graeme Menzies
**111 Places in Whistler
That You Must Not Miss**
ISBN 978-3-7408-1046-7

Floriana Petersen, Steve Werney
**111 Places in San Francisco
That You Must Not Miss**
ISBN 978-3-7408-1698-8

Laurel Moglen, Julia Posey,
Lyudmila Zotova
111 Places in Los Angeles
That You Must Not Miss
ISBN 978-3-7408-1889-0

Jo-Anne Elikann, Susan Lusk
**111 Places in New York
That You Must Not Miss**
ISBN 978-3-7408-1888-3

Evan Levy, Rachel Mazor,
Joost Heijmenberg
**111 Places for Kids in New York
That You Must Not Miss**
ISBN 978-3-7408-1218-8

Wendy Lubovich, Ed Lefkowicz
**111 Museums in New York
That You Must Not Miss**
ISBN 978-3-7408-0379-7

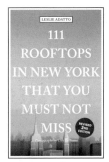

Leslie Adatto, Clay Williams
**111 Rooftops in New York
That You Must Not Miss**
ISBN 978-3-7408-0905-8

Joe DiStefano, Clay Williams
111 Places in Queens
That You Must Not Miss
ISBN 978-3-7408-0020-8

John Major, Ed Lefkowicz
111 Places in Brooklyn
That You Must Not Miss
ISBN 978-3-7408-0380-3

Kevin C. Fitzpatrick Joe Conzo
111 Places in the Bronx
That You Must Not Miss
ISBN 978-3-7408-0492-3

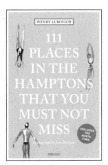

Wendy Lubovich, Jean Hodgens
111 Places in the Hamptons
That You Must Not Miss
ISBN 978-3-7408-1891-3

Andréa Seiger, John Dean
111 Places in Washington
That You Must Not Miss
ISBN 978-3-7408-1890-6

Kaitlin Calogera, Rebecca Grawl,
Cynthia Schiavetto Staliunas
111 Places in Women's
History in Washington
That You Must Not Miss
ISBN 978-3-7408-1590-5

Allison Robicelli, John Dean
111 Places in Baltimore
That You Must Not Miss
ISBN 978-3-7408-0158-8

Kim Windyka, Heather Kapplow,
Alyssa Wood
111 Places in Boston
That You Must Not Miss
ISBN 978-3-7408-1558-5

Amy Bizzarri, Susie Inverso
111 Places in Chicago
That You Must Not Miss
ISBN 978-3-7408-1030-6

Amy Bizzarri, Susie Inverso
111 Places for Kids in Chicago
That You Must Not Miss
ISBN 978-3-7408-0599-9

Michelle Madden, Janet McMillan
111 Places in Milwaukee
That You Must Not Miss
ISBN 978-3-7408-0491-6

Sandra Gurvis, Mitch Geiser
111 Places in Columbus
That You Must Not Miss
ISBN 978-3-7408-0600-2

Cristyle Egitto, Jakob Takos
111 Places in Palm Beach
That You Must Not Miss
ISBN 978-3-7408-1452-6

Travis Swann Taylor
111 Places in Atlanta
That You Must Not Miss
ISBN 978-3-7408-1887-6

Dana DuTerroil, Joni Fincham,
Daniel Jackson
111 Places in Houston
That You Must Not Miss
ISBN 978-3-7408-1697-1

Kelsey Roslin, Nic Yeager,
Jesse Pitzler
111 Places in Austin
That You Must Not Miss
ISBN 978-3-7408-1642-1

Elizabeth Lenell-Davies,
Anita Genua, Claire Davenport
111 Places in Toronto
That You Must Not Miss
ISBN 978-3-7408-0257-8

Jennifer Bain, Christina Ryan
111 Places in Calgary
That You Must Not Miss
ISBN 978-3-7408-0749-8

Photo Credits

All photos by Cortney Kelley except:

Colman Pool (ch. 16): Courtesy Wendy Van De Sompele, courtesy of Seattle Parks & Recreation

FareStart Restaurant (ch. 30): Courtesy of FareStart

KEXP Gathering Space (ch. 55): Dusty Henry (top), Melissa Wax (bottom), courtesy of KEXP

SODO Track Art (ch. 90): Photo by Christopher Derek Bruno (top); Photo by Anna Kooris (bottom)

Suzzallo Library (ch. 97): Alanya Cannon, courtesy of the University of Washington

Woody Guthrie's Legacy (ch. 109): Courtesy of the Museum of Pop Culture, Seattle, WA

Art Credits

Eyes on the World (ch. 4): Richard C. Elliott

30,000 FEET (ch. 9): Brad A. Miller

Late for the Interurban (ch. 54): by Kevin Pettelle

Maury Island UFO Incident Mural (ch. 64): Zach and Nancy Pahl

Exterior Intervention 1: angle of incidence (ch. 90, top): Christopher Derek Bruno, 120 ft. x 45 ft. x 30 ft: Latex on corrugated steel

Balance (ch. 90, bottom): Jillian Evelyn

Odd, I know, but I must thank the pandemic, without which I wouldn't have stayed put long enough to research and rediscover these wonderful places in my city. My husband, Ross, and many friends went on "We're going *where?*" exploratory visits and shared great tips. Interns Sydney Jackson and Nichole Bascue are excellent team players. Thanks to the people who opened doors and shared stories. Thanks to editor Karen Seiger, who paired me with talented photographer Cortney Kelley, who is now a friend. And thanks, Mom, for suggesting I always check that I'm a person and not a pair of pants.
Harriet Baskas

First and foremost, the deepest gratitude to my family. To my husband Philip Kelley, for always believing in me and my slightly absurd ideas. To my kids and grand-daughter, Emmett Kelley, Morgan and Riann Kelley, for your loving support, excitement for this project, and flexibility as my schedule spiraled all over the calendar. And to Austin Kelley, you will forever be a source of inspiration, and deeply nestled into the core of my heart. I will continue to explore the places you never made it to… To Harriet Baskas for curating such a wildly delightful list of featured places, and for your sweet friendship. It has been wonderful adventuring around Seattle with you, especially during the craziness of this pandemic! To Karen Seiger, our solid editor, who nurtured the creative freedom, allowing this book to burst to life. To Kevin Boyer, for being a master connector, who's serendipitous conversation in NYC led this project my way. To the many passionate folks featured within the pages of this book, thank you for letting us into your "thing." Your pride and joyfulness were absolutely contagious! To Seattle, you are a gem beyond compare, and I'm so grateful to live in the PNW.
Cortney Kelley

Harriet Baskas is an author and journalist who has produced radio documentaries on everything from early cowgirls to offbeat museums and written 8 books about unusual attractions, hidden museum treasures and airports around the world. She served as the general manager of three community radio stations in the Pacific Northwest and now reports on travel and the arts for a variety of national outlets and for her blog, StuckatTheAirport.com.

Cortney Kelley, having lived in the PNW for all but four years of her life, is most at home in the dense treescape with the smell of salt water in the air. Primarily a portrait artist, she sensed that the exploration of Seattle couldn't have come at a better time with COVID limitations in full swing, allowing for a deep dive into a city she adores. Nurturing her wanderlust, she is always dreaming and planning the next adventure, camera in tow.